W9-AGG-298

The
INSTANT POT®
Holiday Cookbook

The
INSTANT POT®
Holiday Cookbook

100 FESTIVE RECIPES
TO CELEBRATE THE SEASON

HEATHER SCHLUETER

STERLING EPICURE
New York

STERLING EPICURE
New York

An Imprint of Sterling Publishing Co., Inc.
1166 Avenue of the Americas
New York, NY 10036

STERLING EPICURE is a registered trademark and the distinctive Sterling Epicure logo is a trademark of Sterling Publishing Co., Inc.

Text © 2018 Heather Schlueter
Cover and interior food photography © 2018 Sterling Publishing Co., Inc.

INSTANT POT is a registered trademark and the distinctive Instant Pot logo is a trademark of Double Insight, Inc. and are used with permission of Double Insight, Inc.

All rights reserved. No part of this publication may be reproduced, stored in a retrieval system, or transmitted in any form or by any means (including electronic, mechanical, photocopying, recording, or otherwise) without prior written permission from the publisher.

ISBN 978-1-4549-3313-7

Distributed in Canada by Sterling Publishing Co., Inc.
c/o Canadian Manda Group, 664 Annette Street
Toronto, Ontario M6S 2C8, Canada
Distributed in the United Kingdom by GMC Distribution Services
Castle Place, 166 High Street, Lewes, East Sussex BN7 1XU, England
Distributed in Australia by NewSouth Books
45 Beach Street, Coogee, NSW 2034, Australia

For information about custom editions, special sales, and premium and corporate purchases, please contact Sterling Special Sales at 800-805-5489 or specialsales@sterlingpublishing.com.

Manufactured in Canada

2 4 6 8 10 9 7 5 3 1

sterlingpublishing.com

Cover photograph: © Johnny Autry/Offset.com; Pot illustration in burst by Erna Trani/Shutterstock.com; interior food photography by Bill Milne; Creative Market (Damask pattern): xvi, 20, 52, 84, 114, 128, 148, 176
Cover design David Ter-Avanesyan
Interior design by Janet Evans-Scanlon

To my amazing family,
who make every gathering
feel like a holiday.
I am truly blessed.

CONTENTS

FOREWORD ix

INTRODUCTION x

The Perfect Beginning:
APPETIZERS & STARTERS 1

The Main Event:
**TRADITIONAL &
ALTERNATIVE ENTRÉES** 21

**SPECTACULAR SIDES,
SAUCES & DRESSINGS** 53

A Happy Ending:
DESSERTS 85

WARM WINTER DRINKS 115

ROCK STAR LEFTOVERS 129

GIFTS FROM THE KITCHEN 149

ABOUT THE AUTHOR 168

ACKNOWLEDGMENTS 169

INDEX 170

FOREWORD

The holidays are a time for family, fun, and of course . . . food! Holiday gatherings come in all shapes and sizes, from small and intimate to huge buffet-style shindigs to warm and inviting dinner parties for friends and family—and the food is invariably the focal point of all these get-togethers. The Instant Pot® and this cookbook make it easy for you to put out an impressive spread no matter the size of your holiday affair.

I often call my Instant Pots (yes, I have several) my little problem solvers. Holiday cooking can present a few problems—not enough room in your oven or cook top to cook everything, no practical way to keep meals warm as people work their way through the food line, and an overworked oven that heats up an already hot kitchen. Well, my friends, this appliance solves all those problems! Not only that, I've even included a few recipes that only use the sauté function because it frees up your cooktop and is simple to use! Oh, and let's not overlook how it makes cleanup a breeze. All you need is one pot, a little soap and water, and BAM! you're ready for more amazing culinary creations.

Need to make a turkey but don't want to tie up your oven for hours and hours? Check. Need an elegant appetizer that comes together in just a few minutes? Check. How about some fabulous self-serve warm winter cocktails for your guests? Yep, we've got that covered, too. And of course, don't forget how easy it is now to make perfect, classic mashed potatoes. Yes, indeed, this miracle pot has most definitely made being "the hostess with the mostess" a reality. I wish I had one of these years ago when I first dipped my toe into the party-hosting waters.

In this book, you'll find 100 tried and true classic and alternative holiday eats, treats, and drinks. There's a little something for everyone—appetizers for all occasions, main dishes that will please even the most finicky guests, desserts to die for, must-try warm cocktails and drinks, great ways to use your leftovers, and even fun and creative holiday gifts to make in the kitchen. Grab your appliance and be prepared to amaze your guests with these easy, delicious, creative, and classic holiday treats. And most importantly, enjoy your family and friends throughout the holiday season and beyond. Happy cooking and happy eating and, of course, happy holidays!

—HEATHER SCHLUETER

INTRODUCTION

Tips for Instant Pot Success

The Instant Pot appliance is such a wonderful addition to your arsenal of tools that make holiday cooking easy and convenient. It will save time, as well as oven and cook top space, and it'll make quick work of cleanup. There is a bit of a learning curve, but jump right on it and you'll become an expert in no time!

Following are some of my tips and tricks for getting delicious results every time you use the Instant Pot to make your holiday meals.

It Takes Some Time to Come to Pressure

It's true, Instant Pot multicookers cook meals far faster than traditional cooking methods. But it is important to keep in mind that it takes time for the appliance to build pressure. Some recipes are a bit misleading in that they only list the cooking time. Depending on the temperature and volume of food in the inner pot, pressurization time can be anywhere from a couple of minutes to more than 15 minutes. Cooking time begins after the Instant Pot display reads "on," as it comes to full pressure. Next, the pressure-keeping time will appear once the appliance has reached full pressure. To help you plan accordingly, I have provided "hands-on time" (food prep time), "cooking time" (the amount of time to set the LED display to cook), and "total time," which includes pressurization and release times.

Consider Buying Additional Silicone Rings

Silicone is wonderful. It creates the perfect airtight seal that is necessary for proper pressure-cooking in the appliance. That being said, silicone has a tendency to absorb odors from cooked foods. Some users, including me, choose to purchase additional silicone sealing rings, and switch them out when making savory or sweet dishes. Additional silicone rings can be found on the internet, but I recommend that you use only genuine Instant Pot silicone rings, as using other rings will void your warranty. (Check your appliance manual for all the details.) When purchasing silicone rings for your appliance, be sure to choose the right size for the lid on your appliance.

The Pot Has a Lid Holder

The slots on the side handles of the device double as a resting place for the lid on some models. When the lid is off, the two plastic extensions at the base of the handle fit perfectly into those slots, securely holding the lid at a 90-degree angle. Genius!

Altitude *Does* Make a Difference

If you are using the appliance at high altitude, you will need to increase cooking times by a few minutes. At 5,000 feet, increase cooking time by 15 percent. Add 5 percent cooking time for each additional 1,000 feet.

Protect Your Cabinets from Pressure

The appliance releases steam from the pressure valve on the lid at the end of the cooking cycle. Although the valve is on the back of the lid, be aware of the effect that exposure to steam may have on low-hanging, overhead cabinets. Over time, repeated exposure to steam can discolor the underside or face of your kitchen cabinets. To avoid this, simply rotate the unit and pull it to the edge of the counter so that the release valve is not directly under your cabinets.

What's with All Those Buttons?

At first glance an Instant Pot multicooker can be a little intimidating. But it doesn't take long to realize that the genius of the appliance lies in its simplicity. All of the buttons are presets and designed to make cooking simple. Though preset settings have determined times, cooking modes, and pressure levels, the settings can be changed manually by pressing the buttons repeatedly until the desired setting is reached.

Following is a brief description of each function button, which you'll also find in the manual. Please refer to the manual for your specific appliance, since the buttons on each can vary from model to model.

DISPLAY PANEL

This panel indicates time, mode, and pressure level. The "Less," "Normal," and "More" indicator represents the temperature. The "Low" and "High" indicator represents cooking mode. The vast majority of pressure-cooking is done at normal mode and high pressure.

SOUP/BROTH

Defaults to 30 minutes at normal cooking mode and high pressure. Press the button again to change to low pressure for broth and clear soups.

MEAT/STEW

Defaults to 35 minutes at normal cooking mode and high pressure.

BEAN/CHILI

Defaults to 30 minutes at normal cooking mode and high pressure.

CAKE

Defaults to 40 minutes at normal cooking mode and high pressure.

EGG

Defaults to 5 minutes at normal cooking mode and high pressure.

SLOW COOK

Defaults to 4 hours at normal cooking mode.

SAUTÉ

Defaults to 30 minutes at normal cooking mode.

RICE

This is a fully automated program for white rice only and cannot be altered. It senses the amount of rice in the inner pot and will adjust the time automatically. It is set to low pressure.

MULTIGRAIN

Defaults to 40 minutes at normal cooking mode and high pressure. Selecting the "More" mode will enable a 45-minute pre-soak warm cycle.

PORRIDGE

Defaults to 20 minutes at normal cooking mode and high pressure.

STEAM

Defaults to 10 minutes at normal cooking mode and high pressure.

STERILIZE

Defaults to 30 minutes at normal cooking mode and low pressure. Used to sterilize canning equipment and baby bottles, among other things.

YOGURT

Defaults to boil at high cooking mode for 8 hours.

PRESSURE COOK (MANUAL on some models)

Defaults to 35 minutes at normal cooking mode and high pressure. This is the most used button, and you will likely change the time for this one frequently.

PRESSURE LEVEL

Press this to toggle the between low and high.

DELAY START

This can be set to delay the start of any function.

KEEP WARM

This will automatically engage at the end of a cooking cycle and can be turned off manually by pressing the cancel button.

CANCEL

This is the "Off" button. Press this to turn the unit off or to turn off one function before switching to another function.

"+" AND "−"

These are used to adjust the cooking time after a cooking function has been selected.

My Cooking Suggestions

Here are a few basic ideas to keep in mind as you prepare holiday meals with your appliance.

CORNSTARCH IS YOUR FRIEND

It takes additional liquid in a pressure-cooking recipe for the pot to come to full pressure, which can lead to a thinner sauce. If, at the end of the cooking cycle, you would like a thicker sauce, simply mix a couple of tablespoons of cornstarch (or potato flakes) with a couple of tablespoons of water to make a slurry. Once the dish is fully cooked, turn on the sauté function, let the liquid come to a boil, add the slurry, and stir the mixture until the desired thickness is reached.

LEARN THE THREE TYPES OF PRESSURE RELEASE

The recipes in this book call for different types of pressure releases.
Learn the differences to achieve the best results.

QUICK RELEASE As soon as the pressure-keeping time reaches zero, turn the steam release handle to the Venting position to let steam out until the float valve drops down and you no longer hear steam coming out. Never pull out the steam release handle while releasing steam, as escaping steam is extremely hot and can scald. Additionally, avoid putting your hands directly over the release valve.

NATURAL RELEASE After the pressure-keeping time reaches zero, allow the cooker to cool naturally until the float valve drops down. Depending on the type and quantity of food inside the inner pot, a full natural release can take anywhere from about 10 minutes to up to an hour. Many recipes call for natural release for a period of time (for example, "natural release for 15 minutes"). This allows some of the pressure to release on its own. After the prescribed natural release time, you can then turn the valve to the Venting position to release the remaining pressure.

SLOW RELEASE For foods that contain a lot of starch, such as pastas or beans, a slow release is often suggested, because the steam inside the appliance will collect a fair amount of starch. During a quick release, starch may come through the valve, which can cause spitting and create a bit of a mess. For a slow release, turn the pressure valve toward the Venting position, but not all the way at once. Turn the valve just a little bit and hold it stationary as the pressure releases and the valve stops spitting. To keep your hands clear of the steam release valve, use a long-handled spoon or spatula instead. As the pressure releases, turn the valve a little bit more toward the Venting position. Continue this method until all the pressure has been fully released.

CRISP THINGS UP IN AN OVEN OR ON THE GRILL

The Instant Pot multicooker cooks with pressure and steam, resulting in meat that is fall-off-the-bone tender and dishes that can be cooked very quickly, but one thing it can't do is make food crunchy or crispy. So if you're looking for golden-brown, crispy turkey skin, or a nice char on your chicken wings, make sure to pop the meat into a hot oven or onto a hot grill for a couple of minutes after the pressure-cooking process.

DO NOT OVERFILL THE INNER POT

There is a "²⁄₃" marker on the inside of the inner pot of your appliance. Use it as a guide so that you don't overfill the inner pot. If you fill it with ingredients past this line, there will not be enough space within the inner pot for pressure to build and seal properly. I have found that there are a few exceptions to this—if you are stacking smaller dishes such as ramekins and mini springform pans in the pot, the height of the stack can exceed the ²⁄₃ line, because there will be enough space around it to enable proper pressure and sealing. If you are cooking starchy ingredients that will foam, such as rice or beans, make sure to not exceed the ½ line.

MAKE SURE THE BOTTOM IS CLEAN

Some recipes call for ingredients to be sautéed before pressure-cooking, and the Instant Pot multicooker allows you to do that without using another pot or pan. However, if you use this highly praised feature, it can leave brown bits on the bottom of the inner pot, which is great for the flavor of your dish, but if the bottom is coated with those brown bits or a thick paste, the appliance will not seal properly. This is why it is critical to deglaze the inner pot and scrape the bottom clean with a wooden spoon or spatula before switching from sautéing to pressure cooking.

DIFFERENT BRANDS OF INGREDIENTS MAY PRODUCE DIFFERENT RESULTS

This is true for all types of cooking, but it is particularly relevant to Instant Pot cooking. Depending on the brand you use, the results may differ. For example, salt can have very different levels of "saltiness." So when one brand is used, it may produce the perfect result for your taste, but another brand may produce an overly salty taste. This is true of many products—flour has a range of textures (some types are heavier or lighter than others), a difference that might produce unexpected results—a sauce that is too "thin" or one that's too thick and interferes with proper sealing of the pot. This is also true of various brands of rice, which may have different levels of starch. Don't be afraid to experiment with different brands to ensure that you get exactly the results you want, and then stick with them to get perfectly consistent results every time! It's well worth the effort.

POT-IN-POT COOKING METHOD

The versatility of the Instant Pot multicooker is one of the reasons why it is so popular. Many dishes that are usually baked in an oven can be cooked much faster in the appliance using the "Pot-In-Pot" method. A casserole or a dessert can be placed in a baking dish (such as a ramekin) or a pan (such as a springform pan) that is smaller than the inner pot of the appliance. The smaller dish is placed on the steam rack inside the inner pot of the appliance, which allows the dish to be cooked without being submerged in the liquid required to bring the appliance to pressure.

If the smaller dish within the inner pot is a tight squeeze, simply use aluminum foil to create a "sling" that will allow you to lower and raise the dish without using your fingers to get the smaller pot in and out. To make the sling, cut off a piece of aluminum foil approximately 20 inches (50 centimeters) long, and fold it lengthwise several times to form a 3-inch (8 cm) wide strip of foil that is 20 inches (50 cm) long. Place this strip under the bottom and up the sides of the dish you are placing on the steam rack inside the inner pot of the appliance. Use the ends of the foil as "handles" to lower and raise the dish. Just make sure to tuck the ends fully inside the appliance when you put on the lid so it does not interfere with the normal sealing process.

THE INSTANT POT ACCU SLIM SOUS VIDE IMMERSION CIRCULATOR ADDS EVEN MORE VERSATILITY

The sous vide method of cooking is used by many high-end restaurants to achieve perfectly cooked food, particularly meat. Food is put into an airtight bag, which is then submerged in a "water bath" that is held at the cooking temperature as the water circulates over a certain length of time. This results in food that is evenly cooked from front to back and end to end at the exact desired temperature. Meats that are cooked by the sous vide method are then typically seared in a very hot skillet for a few seconds on each side, giving them a nice crust without overcooking the outer portion of the food. If you're looking for perfection, give this method a try. It requires the Instant Pot Accu Slim Sous Vide Immersion Circulator but is well worth it.

JUST BECAUSE YOU CAN COOK IT IN THE APPLIANCE DOESN'T MEAN YOU SHOULD

All the conveniences of the Instant Pot multicooker may lead you to believe that you can cook anything in it, but in reality some types of food are better served by cooking them in the traditional manner—a flavorful ribeye steak is still best cooked in a cast iron skillet or on a very hot grill (or with the sous vide method); delicate beef tenderloin should still be roasted in the oven. And crispy egg rolls? Yes, they still need frying. Although it is very tempting to throw anything and everything into the appliance, stick to what works best, and you and your family, friends, and holiday guests will love the results!

TAKE ADVANTAGE OF THE SAUTÉ FUNCTION

The sauté function is one of the most useful options of the Instant Pot. Yes, it's perfect for browning meats before pressure cooking, but it's also great when your stovetop is filled with other holiday creations and you're looking for a place to sear, heat, or warm up another dish. It's quick, simple, and super-easy to use, and it even works as a double boiler. I have included some recipes in this cookbook that only use the Sauté button, so you too can take advantage of this wonderfully convenient function.

The Perfect Beginning

APPETIZERS & STARTERS

Warm Brie with
Honey & Apples 2

Salted Boiled Peanuts 3

Tender Stuffed
Mushrooms 5

Caramelized Onion
& Cranberry Dip 7

Buffalo Chicken Dip 8

Warm & Creamy
Spinach Artichoke Dip 10

Holiday Hummus 11

Classic Deviled Eggs 12

Asian Chicken Wings 14

Bourbon-Glazed
Meatballs the Easy Way 17

Shrimp with
Butter & Garlic 19

Sweet & Spicy
Cocktail Sausages 19

WARM BRIE WITH HONEY & APPLES

YIELD: 12 Servings
HANDS-ON TIME: 5 Minutes
COOKING TIME: 4 Minutes
TOTAL TIME: 15 Minutes
BUTTONS TO USE: Pressure Cook
RELEASE TYPE: Quick Release

Start the evening off right with warm, creamy Brie drizzled with honey and served with sliced apples and elegant crackers. You will need a 7-inch (18 cm) ovenproof baking dish or spring-form pan for this recipe. (See "Pot-in-Pot Cooking Method" on page xiv.)

1 (16-ounce) (450 g) wheel of fresh Brie cheese

2 tablespoons high-quality honey

3 green apples, thinly sliced

crackers of choice for serving

Place the wheel of Brie into a 7-inch-wide (18 cm) baking dish. Place the Instant Pot steam rack into the Instant Pot inner pot and add 1 cup (240 ml) of water. Place the baking dish on top of the steam rack. Select the Pressure Cook button and set the time to 4 minutes.

When cooking is complete, turn the valve toward venting to release all the pressure.

Carefully remove the baking dish using oven mitts. Transfer the warm Brie to a serving platter. Drizzle honey over the warm cheese and serve it with sliced apples and crackers.

SALTED BOILED PEANUTS

YIELD: 1 Pound (450 g) Peanuts

HANDS-ON TIME: 5 Minutes

COOKING TIME: 75 Minutes

TOTAL TIME: 120 Minutes

BUTTONS TO USE: Pressure Cook

RELEASE TYPE: Natural Release

Although boiled peanuts are a traditional Southern snack, they are now being served everywhere in the country, thanks to the Instant Pot, so jump on the bandwagon!

1 pound (450 g) raw peanuts in the shell

½ cup (140 g) Kosher salt

Rinse the peanuts in a colander under running water. Remove any pieces of debris.

Place the peanuts and salt in the Instant Pot inner pot and pour in enough water to cover the peanuts. Stir well. The peanuts will float so you may have to weigh them down with an ovenproof steam rack.

Secure the lid, ensuring the valve is turned to the Sealing position. Press the Pressure Cook button and set the time to 75 minutes.

When cooking is complete, let the pot sit another 30 minutes and then turn the valve to the Venting position to release any remaining pressure.

Pour the peanuts into a colander to drain. Toss the peanuts with more kosher salt, if you like, and then transfer the peanuts to a paper-lined plate or paper bag.

TENDER STUFFED MUSHROOMS

YIELD: 25 Mushrooms

HANDS-ON TIME: 10 Minutes

COOKING TIME: 5 Minutes

TOTAL TIME: 20 Minutes

BUTTONS TO USE: Sauté and Pressure Cook

RELEASE TYPE: Quick Release

This classic appetizer is always a crowd-pleaser. Warm and tender mushrooms stuffed with tangy Romano cheese and sautéed mushroom bits make this pop-in-your-mouth appetizer perfect for any type of dinner party. If you want to brown the tops of these delicate appetizers, simply pop them under a hot broiler for a few minutes when they are done cooking. You will need a shallow 7-inch-wide (18 cm) ovenproof baking dish that fits in your Instant Pot multicooker. (See "Pot-in-Pot Cooking Method" on page xiv.)

2 tablespoons butter

25 jumbo white mushrooms, stems removed, stems chopped into small pieces and reserved

1 clove garlic

½ cup (55 g) dried bread crumbs

½ cup (45 g) Romano cheese, freshly grated

2 tablespoons Italian parsley, chopped

3 tablespoons olive oil, optional

chopped Italian parsley for serving

Press the Sauté button to heat up the Instant Pot inner pot. When the display reads "Hot," add the butter, mushroom stem pieces, and garlic. Stir the mixture until the mushrooms just begin to give off their juices, approximately 3–4 minutes. Add the breadcrumbs and stir until well combined. Press Cancel to turn off sauté function.

Pour the mushroom stem mixture into a medium bowl and add the cheese and parsley. Stir to combine. Stuff the mushroom caps with the bread crumb mixture, making sure to mound the mixture so that it rises above the edges of the mushroom caps.

continued

Carefully place the stuffed mushrooms into the baking dish in a single layer. Cover the dish with aluminum foil.

Clean out the Instant Pot inner pot and then place it back inside the appliance. Put the Instant Pot steam rack into the Instant Pot inner pot and add 1 cup (240 ml) of water. Place the baking dish on top of the steam rack. Secure the lid, ensuring the valve is turned to the Sealing position. Press the Pressure Cook button and set the time to 5 minutes.

When cooking is complete, turn the valve to the Venting position to release the pressure. Remove the lid and carefully take out the baking dish. Remove the foil from baking dish.

If you want to brown the tops of the mushrooms, drizzle them with olive oil and place the dish under a hot broiler for 5–10 minutes, until the tops of the mushrooms are golden. Garnish with chopped parsley and serve the mushrooms while they are warm.

CARAMELIZED ONION & CRANBERRY DIP

YIELD: 25 Servings
HANDS-ON TIME: 5 Minutes
COOKING TIME: 15 Minutes
TOTAL TIME: 25 Minutes
BUTTONS TO USE: Pressure Cook
RELEASE TYPE: Quick Release

Serve this dip with a crusty baguette and a side of soft goat cheese for a sweet and tangy festive appetizer.

Place all the ingredients, except the goat cheese, sliced baguette, and the slurry into the Instant Pot inner pot and stir well. Secure the lid, ensuring the valve is turned to the Sealing position. Press the Pressure Cook button and set the time to 10 minutes.

When cooking is complete, turn the valve toward the Venting position to release all the pressure. Remove the lid and stir.

Depending on the water content of the apples, the mixture may be a bit thin. If it is too thin, press the Sauté button and add the slurry. Stir the mixture until the desired consistency is reached.

To serve, spread the goat cheese on slices of the baguette, and then top the cheese with the onion and cranberry mixture.

2 large sweet onions, peeled and sliced into ½-inch (1 cm) slices

2 tart apples, peeled, seeded, and cut into ½-inch (1 cm) slices

2 cups (200 g) fresh cranberries

¼ cup (60 ml) apple cider

¼ cup (60 ml) balsamic vinegar

8 ounces (225 g) soft goat cheese for serving

a crusty baguette, sliced for serving

1 tablespoon water mixed with 1 tablespoon cornstarch for the slurry, if needed

BUFFALO CHICKEN DIP

YIELD: 4 Cups (950 ml)

HANDS-ON TIME: 5 Minutes

COOKING TIME: 10 Minutes

TOTAL TIME: 20 Minutes

BUTTONS TO USE: Pressure Cook

RELEASE TYPE: Quick Release

Serving up a creamy, cheesy, tender chicken dip that has just the right amount of heat is a great way to get the party started! You will need a 1-quart ovenproof baking dish that will fit in your Instant Pot for this dish. (See "Pot-in-Pot Cooking Method" on page xiv.)

In a large bowl, mix together the chicken, cream cheese, pepper sauce, ranch dressing, and ½ cup (68 g) of the blue cheese. Put the mixture into a 1-quart (1 liter) ovenproof dish. Top the mixture with the rest of the blue cheese crumbles, and cover the dish with aluminum foil.

Place the Instant Pot steam rack in the Instant Pot inner pot and add 1 cup (240 ml) of water. Place the baking dish on top of the steam rack. Secure the lid, ensuring the valve is turned to the Sealing position. Press the Pressure Cook button and set the time to 10 minutes.

When cooking is complete, turn the valve to the Venting position to release the pressure. Remove the lid.

Carefully remove the baking dish using oven mitts. Remove the foil and top the chicken dip with the green onions. Serve hot with celery, carrots, and crackers.

2 cups (250 g) cooked, shredded chicken

1 (8-ounce) (225 g) package cream cheese, room temperature

½ cup (120 ml) pepper sauce of choice (such as Frank's®) or Buffalo sauce

½ cup (120 ml) ranch dressing

1 cup (135 g) blue cheese crumbles, divided

2 green onions, green parts only, sliced crosswise for topping

TIP: It is very easy to cook a whole chicken in the Instant Pot and use it in a variety of recipes. To make shredded chicken, season a whole chicken with salt and pepper, place the steam rack in the Instant Pot inner pot, and pour 1 cup (240 ml) of water into the pot. Place the chicken (standing on one end) on top of the steam rack. Secure the lid, ensuring the valve is turned toward Sealing, and press the Pressure Cook button. Set the time to 30 minutes. When cooking is complete, let the pot sit another 5–10 minutes, then turn the valve toward Venting to release any remaining pressure. Remove the lid and, using tongs, carefully transfer the chicken to a cutting board. Use two forks to shred the chicken, and use it in any recipe that calls for cooked chicken. It is the perfect method for making Buffalo Chicken Dip.

WARM & CREAMY SPINACH ARTICHOKE DIP

YIELD: 12 Servings

HANDS-ON TIME: 5 Minutes

COOKING TIME: 10 Minutes

TOTAL TIME: 20 Minutes

BUTTONS TO USE: Pressure Cook

RELEASE TYPE: Quick Release

To finish this delightfully creamy dip, simply top it with some mozzarella and pop it under a hot broiler for a few minutes after the cooking process is complete. Serve it with a thinly sliced baguette. You will need a 7-inch-wide (18 cm) ovenproof baking dish that fits in your Instant Pot. (See "Pot-in-Pot Cooking Method" on page xiv.)

In a large bowl, combine all ingredients except the mozzarella and mix well. Spray the baking dish with cooking spray. Pour the mixture into the baking dish and cover it with aluminum foil.

Place the Instant Pot steam rack into the Instant Pot inner pot and add 1 cup (240 ml) of water. Place the baking dish on top of the steam rack. Secure the lid, ensuring the valve is turned to the Sealing position. Press the Pressure Cook button and set the time to 10 minutes.

When cooking is complete, turn the valve to the Venting position to release the pressure. Remove the lid and carefully remove the baking dish. Remove the foil from the baking dish.

OPTIONAL: Sprinkle mozzarella over the top of the dip and place under a hot broiler for 5–10 minutes, until the top is golden brown. Serve the dip with crunchy, toasted baguette slices.

cooking spray

1 (10-ounce) (284 g) package frozen spinach, thawed and well-drained

1 (14-ounce) (400 g) can artichoke hearts, drained and chopped

8 ounces (225 g) cream cheese, room temperature

½ cup (45 g) Parmesan cheese

¼ cup (60 g) sour cream

¼ cup (60 g) mayonnaise

½ teaspoon red pepper flakes

1 garlic glove, finely minced

½ cup (60 g) shredded mozzarella for topping, optional

toasted baguette slices, for serving

HOLIDAY HUMMUS

YIELD: 4 Cups (950 ml)

HANDS-ON TIME: 5 Minutes

COOKING TIME: 50 Minutes

TOTAL TIME: 75 Minutes

BUTTONS TO USE: Bean/Chili

RELEASE TYPE: Natural Release

Roasted red peppers and diced cucumbers give this appetizer holiday flair. You will need a food processor or a stand blender for this recipe.

2 cups (360 g) dried chickpeas (also called garbanzo beans)

3 garlic cloves, peeled and smashed

1 tablespoon vegetable oil

1 teaspoon salt

½ teaspoon pepper

¾ cup (180 ml) olive oil, divided

1 (16-ounce) (475 g) jar roasted red peppers, drained and divided

½ small cucumber, diced

pita chips, for serving

Place the chickpeas, garlic, and vegetable oil in the Instant Pot inner pot. Add 6 cups (1.5 liters) of water and stir. Secure the lid, ensuring the valve is turned to the Sealing position. Press the Bean/Chili button and set the time to 50 minutes.

When cooking is complete, let the pot sit 10 minutes, and then turn the valve to the Venting position to release remaining pressure. Remove the lid. Drain the chickpeas into a colander over a large bowl to capture the cooking liquid for later use.

Once drained, combine the chickpeas, salt, pepper, 4 tablespoons of the olive oil, ¾ of the red peppers, and ½ cup (120 ml) of the reserved cooking liquid in a food processor. Pulse the food processor to blend the ingredients, and then turn the processor to high. Slowly add the remaining olive oil and additional reserved cooking liquid, as needed, to reach the desired consistency.

Chop the remaining peppers into small bite-size pieces.

Serve the hummus with a drizzle of olive oil and a mound of diced cucumber in the middle. Top the hummus with the remaining diced red peppers and serve with pita chips.

TIP: Hummus will thicken quite a bit as it cools, so make it just a bit thinner and the consistency will be perfect for serving to your guests.

CLASSIC DEVILED EGGS

YIELD: 12 Deviled Egg Halves
HANDS-ON TIME: 10 Minutes
COOKING TIME: 7 Minutes
TOTAL TIME: 20 Minutes
BUTTONS TO USE: Pressure Cook
RELEASE TYPE: Quick Release

Everyone loves deviled eggs—and the Instant Pot delivers perfectly cooked ones that practically peel themselves, making it a snap to make these festive eggs any time the spirit moves you.

6 large eggs

¼ cup (60 g) mayonnaise

1 teaspoon mustard

¼ teaspoon salt

¼ teaspoon pepper

Smoked paprika and chopped chives for garnish

Place the Instant Pot steam rack in the Instant Pot inner pot and add 1 cup (240 ml) of water. Place the eggs on top of steam rack (you can also use a steamer basket instead of the steam pot). Secure the lid, ensuring the valve is turned to the Sealing position. Press the Pressure Cook button and set the time to 7 minutes.

When cooking is complete, turn the valve to the Venting position to release the pressure. Remove the lid and remove the eggs with a pair of tongs. Place the eggs in a bowl and fill it with cool water until the eggs are cool enough to handle.

Peel the eggs under running water, pat them dry, and then slice the eggs in half lengthwise.

Remove the egg yolks from the whites and place them in a medium bowl, reserving the whites. Add the mayonnaise, mustard, and the salt and pepper to the yolks and mix well.

Spoon the egg-yolk mixture back into the egg white halves and sprinkle the tops with smoked paprika and chopped chives. Serve the eggs cold or at room temperature.

TIP: Remove the eggs from the Instant Pot as soon as the pressure has been released. Leaving them in any longer can result in overcooked eggs.

ASIAN CHICKEN WINGS

YIELD: 4 Pounds (1.75 kg) Chicken Wings

HANDS-ON TIME: 10 Minutes

COOKING TIME: 5 Minutes

TOTAL TIME: 30 Minutes

BUTTONS TO USE: Pressure Cook

RELEASE TYPE: Natural Release

Tender, fall-off-the-bone wings with a sticky, sweet, and spicy sauce—what partygoer wouldn't love that? Toss these wings under a hot broiler after the cooking phase to give them a nice char.

TO PREPARE THE SAUCE

In a small saucepan, combine all of the sauce ingredients. Whisk the mixture over medium heat until the sugar is dissolved and the sauce begins to thicken. Remove the pan from the heat.

TO PREPARE THE WINGS

Sprinkle the wings with the salt and pepper. Place the wings in the Instant Pot inner pot and drizzle ½ cup (120 ml) of the sauce over the wings. Pour the vinegar into the pot.

Secure the lid, ensuring the valve is turned to the Sealing position. Press the Pressure Cook button and set the time to 5 minutes.

When cooking is complete, let the pot sit for another 10 minutes, and then turn the valve to the Venting position to release any remaining pressure. Remove the lid.

FOR THE SAUCE

½ cup (120 g) ketchup

½ (100 g) cup sugar

½ cup (120 ml) soy sauce

¼ cup (85 g) honey

1 tablespoon hoisin sauce

1 tablespoon minced fresh ginger

2 cloves garlic, minced

1 teaspoon red pepper flakes

FOR THE WINGS

4 pounds (1.75 kg) chicken wings, patted dry

1 tablespoon salt

1 tablespoon pepper

¾ cup (180 ml) vinegar

1 tablespoon sesame seeds for garnish

Carefully remove the wings with a pair of tongs and transfer them to a large bowl. Pour one-half of the remaining sauce on the wings. Gently turn the wings in the sauce to ensure an even coating. Transfer the wings to a rimmed baking sheet and arrange them in a single layer. Turn the oven broiler on high.

Place the baking sheet under the hot broiler for 5–10 minutes or until there's a nice char on the wings. Remove the baking sheet from the broiler, brush the remaining sauce on the wings, and sprinkle the sesame seeds over the top. Serve the wings hot.

TIP: Reduce the amount of red pepper flakes if you want less heat.

BOURBON-GLAZED MEATBALLS THE EASY WAY

YIELD: 10 Servings
HANDS-ON TIME: 2 Minutes
COOKING TIME: 5 Minutes
TOTAL TIME: 10 Minutes
BUTTONS TO USE: Pressure Cook
RELEASE TYPE: Quick Release

Using pre-made frozen meatballs and store-bought barbecue sauce is definitely the fastest way to make these delicious sweet, tangy, and tasty cocktail treats. But if you have a great recipe for homemade meatballs and the time to make them, by all means use them here. There's no need to brown the meatballs first if you're making them from scratch, just don't crowd them together too much in the pot.

1 pound (450 g) frozen meatballs (or use homemade meatballs)

2 cups (480 ml) barbecue sauce (store bought or homemade)

¼ cup (60 ml) bourbon

¼ cup (85 g) honey

chopped chives, for serving

Place all the ingredients in the Instant Pot inner pot and gently stir them together. Secure the lid, ensuring the valve is turned to the Sealing position. Press the Pressure Cook button and set the time to 5 minutes.

When cooking is complete, turn the valve to the Venting position to release the pressure. Open the lid and stir the mixture in order to coat all the meatballs.

Serve the meatballs from the Instant Pot, which should be set to the keep warm function.

SHRIMP WITH BUTTER & GARLIC

YIELD: 10 Servings
HANDS-ON TIME: 5 Minutes
COOKING TIME: 3 Minutes
TOTAL TIME: 10 Minutes
BUTTONS TO USE: Sauté
RELEASE TYPE: None

This quick and elegant appetizer makes the most of the wonderful Instant Pot sauté function—and cleanup is a breeze! Use tail-on shrimp to make this easy finger food for your guests.

4 tablespoons butter

1 clove garlic, minced

1 pound (450 g) (20 count) jumbo tail-on shrimp, shells removed, deveined, but tails left on

lemon wedges for garnish

Press the Sauté button to heat up the Instant Pot inner pot. When the display reads "Hot," add the butter. When the butter has melted, add the garlic and stir the mixture continuously for 1 minute, and then add the shrimp.

Stir the shrimp to coat them evenly with the butter and garlic. Cook them for 2–3 minutes or until they have turned pink. Press the Cancel button to turn off the sauté function and immediately transfer the shrimp to a serving platter. Use the lemon wedges for garnish.

Serve the shrimp with a squeeze of lemon juice, and make sure to have lots of cocktail napkins nearby!

SWEET & SPICY COCKTAIL SAUSAGES

YIELD: 8 Servings
HANDS-ON TIME: 5 Minutes
COOKING TIME: 2 Minutes
TOTAL TIME: 10 Minutes
BUTTONS TO USE: Pressure Cook
RELEASE TYPE: Quick Release

It's always welcoming to have a simple, but very tasty, appetizer waiting for your guests as they arrive. They'll go nuts over these cocktail sausages. This recipe can easily be doubled for a larger group of guests.

2 (12-ounce) (340 g) packages of cocktail sausages

1 cup (240 g) ketchup

¼ cup (85 g) honey

¼ cup (50 g) brown sugar

2 tablespoons apple cider vinegar

1 tablespoon Dijon mustard

½ teaspoon red pepper flakes

½ cup (120 ml) lager beer

Place all the ingredients into the Instant Pot inner pot and stir well. Secure the lid, ensuring the valve is turned to the Sealing position. Press the Pressure Cook button and set the time to 2 minutes.

When cooking is complete, turn the valve to the Venting position to release the pressure. Remove the lid and press the Sauté button. Stir and continue to sauté the mixture until the sauce thickens. Press the Cancel button to turn off the sauté function. Serve the sausages warm.

The Main Event
TRADITIONAL & ALTERNATIVE ENTRÉES

Succulent Glazed Ham 22

Pumpkin & Sausage
Penne 24

Crispy Cornish
Game Hens for Two 25

Red Wine–Braised
Beef Brisket 26

Tender Turkey for a
Small Gathering 29

Beef Pot Roast 31

Colorful Veggie Lasagna 32

Easy Duck à l'Orange 35

Beef Stroganoff 37

Beer-Braised
Shredded Beef 38

Steamed Lobster Tails 39

Roast Pork Loin 41

Venison Roast 42

Turkey Breast for Two 44

Pulled Pork 46

Sous Vide Filet Mignon 47

Sous Vide Seared Tuna 50

SUCCULENT GLAZED HAM

YIELD: 6–7 Pounds (2.75–3.25 kg)

HANDS-ON TIME: 5 Minutes

COOKING TIME: 3 Minutes

TOTAL TIME: 15 Minutes

BUTTONS TO USE: Pressure Cook

RELEASE TYPE: Natural Release

Free up your oven space and make this tender and flavorful ham right in the Instant Pot—in less than 15 minutes! It doesn't get much better than that!

Place the Instant Pot steam rack into the Instant Pot inner pot and add 1 cup (240 ml) of pineapple juice.

Mix the brown sugar, ¼ cup (60 ml) pineapple juice, and the mustard to make the glaze (or use the packet that came with the ham). The glaze should have a paste-like consistency.

Spread the glaze all over the surface of the ham.

Place the ham on top of the steam rack (to make the ham fit in the pot, you might have to stand it on one end).

Secure the lid, ensuring the valve is turned to the Sealing position. Press the Pressure Cook button and set the time to 3 minutes.

When cooking is complete, let the pot sit for 5 minutes, and then turn the valve to the Venting position.

Remove the lid and remove the ham using 2 sets of tongs. Place the ham on a serving platter and spoon the juices from the pot over the top. Garnish the ham with sage and pineapple wedges, if you like.

FOR THE HAM

1 cup (240 ml) pineapple juice (or apple juice)

1 spiral sliced 6–7-pound (2.75–3.25 kg) ham

Sage and pineapple wedges for garnish, if desired

FOR THE GLAZE
(or use the glaze packet that comes with the ham)

½ cup (100 g) brown sugar

¼ cup (60 ml) pineapple juice

2 tablespoons Dijon mustard

PUMPKIN & SAUSAGE PENNE

YIELD: 6 Servings

HANDS-ON TIME: 10 Minutes

COOKING TIME: 4 Minutes

TOTAL TIME: 30 Minutes

BUTTONS TO USE: Sauté and Pressure Cook

RELEASE TYPE: Quick Release

This simple pasta is a perfect seasonal alternative to traditional holiday offerings. Be sure to use canned pumpkin (not pumpkin pie filling!) when you make this recipe.

Select the sauté function to heat the inner pot. Once the display reads "Hot," add the oil. Heat oil for 30 seconds. Add the shallots and sauté for about 3 minutes, or until they soften slightly. Add the garlic and sauté for 1 minute more.

Add the sausage to the pot, stirring and crumbling it with a wooden spoon until it has browned (the meat should not be pink). Add the sage, hot pepper sauce, salt, pepper, and nutmeg. Stir the mixture until it is well combined.

Press Cancel to turn off the sauté function. Add the chicken broth and penne. Stir the mixture until it is well combined.

Secure the lid, ensuring the valve is turned to the Sealing position. Press Pressure Cook and set the time to 4 minutes.

When cooking is complete, turn the valve to the Venting position to let the pressure release. When all the pressure is released, carefully remove the lid. Add the pumpkin puree and the cream. Stir the mixture well.

Press Cancel to turn off the unit. Press Sauté and add the cornstarch and water slurry if you want to thicken the sauce. Stir it for 1–2 minutes until the sauce is thick and creamy.

1 tablespoon vegetable oil

2 medium shallots, minced

2 cloves garlic, minced

1 pound (450 g) ground sweet Italian sausage or 1 pound (450 g) sweet Italian sausages, meat removed from casings

1 tablespoon fresh sage, chopped (or 1 teaspoon dried ground sage)

1 teaspoon hot pepper sauce, such as Tabasco® (optional)

1 teaspoon salt

½ teaspoon freshly ground pepper

⅛ teaspoon ground or grated nutmeg

4 cups (950 ml) chicken broth

1 pound (450 g) uncooked penne pasta

1 (15-ounce) (425 g) can pumpkin puree

½ cup (120 ml) heavy cream

2 tablespoons cornstarch mixed with 2 tablespoons water for slurry to thicken sauce, if needed

CRISPY CORNISH GAME HENS FOR TWO

YIELD: 2 Servings

HANDS-ON TIME: 5 Minutes

COOKING TIME: 25 Minutes

TOTAL TIME: 45 Minutes

BUTTONS TO USE: Pressure Cook

RELEASE TYPE: Natural Release

These game hens are so easy to make, you don't need to save them for a special occasion, but they will most definitely make your holiday dinner for two extra special. For a beautiful crispy skin, finish them off under a hot broiler for 5–10 minutes.

2 Cornish game hens, rinsed and with giblets removed

1 medium onion, peeled and quartered

1 lemon, quartered

2 sprigs fresh rosemary

2 tablespoons butter, softened

1 teaspoon Italian seasoning

½ teaspoon salt

½ teaspoon pepper

Place the Instant Pot steam rack in the Instant Pot inner pot and add 1 cup (240 ml) of water. Carefully place the hens on top of the steam rack, standing them on end, if necessary.

Place the onion, lemon, and rosemary sprigs around the hens.

Secure the lid, ensuring the valve is turned to the Sealing position, and set the time to 25 minutes.

When cooking is complete, let the pot sit for another 5 minutes, and then turn the valve to the Venting position to release any remaining pressure. Remove the lid.

Turn on the oven broiler while the pressure is releasing.

Carefully remove the hens from the pot, using tongs, and set them breast side up on a broiler pan.

Coat the breast side of the hens with the softened butter and sprinkle them with the Italian seasoning, salt, and pepper.

Place the hens under the hot broiler for 5–10 minutes until the skin is crispy and golden brown. Serve immediately.

TIP: You can also use frozen Cornish game hens in this recipe; just add 5 minutes to the pressure-cooking time.

RED WINE-BRAISED BEEF BRISKET

YIELD: 6 Servings
HANDS-ON TIME: 10 Minutes
COOKING TIME: 70 Minutes
TOTAL TIME: 110 Minutes
BUTTONS TO USE: Meat/Stew
RELEASE TYPE: Natural Release

The beef lovers in your family will ooh and aah over this rich, tender, and flavorful beef brisket. Enjoy it with Classic Mashed Potatoes (page 73) and Pomegranate Brussels Sprouts (page 66). And the leftovers are perfect for Beef & Carmelized Onion Sandwiches (page 131).

1 (5–6 pound) (2.25–2.75 kg) beef brisket, fat trimmed to ¼ inch (about .5 cm)

1 teaspoon salt

1 teaspoon freshly ground black pepper

2 tablespoons butter

1 cup (240 ml) dry red wine

1 cup (240 ml) beef broth

2 tablespoons tomato paste

6 cloves garlic, peeled and smashed

2 sprigs fresh rosemary

Italian parsley, chopped, for garnish

Sprinkle the brisket with salt and pepper on all sides.

Press the Sauté button to heat the Instant Pot inner pot. When the display reads "Hot," add the butter to pot. As soon as the butter has melted, sear the meat by placing it fat side–down in the pot. Leave the meat undisturbed for 3–4 minutes, and then turn it over to sear the other side for 2–3 minutes.

Remove the beef from the pot and add the wine to deglaze the bottom of the pot, making sure to scrape up all the brown bits from the bottom, using a wooden spoon. Press Cancel to turn off the sauté function.

Add the beef broth to the pot and whisk in the tomato paste until the mixture is fully blended.

Place the beef back in the pot. Top the meat with the garlic and rosemary. Secure the lid, ensuring the valve is turned to the Sealing position. Press the Meat/Stew button and set the time to 70 minutes.

When cooking is complete, let the pot sit for another 20 minutes, and then turn the valve to the Venting position to release any remaining pressure.

Transfer the brisket to a serving platter and tent it with foil.

Press the Sauté button and whisk together the remaining liquid. Bring the liquid to a boil and allow it to simmer for 10 minutes in order to reduce the sauce a bit. Add additional salt and pepper to taste.

Slice the brisket and drizzle some of the sauce over the top. Use the chopped parsley for garnish.

TENDER TURKEY FOR A SMALL GATHERING

YIELD: 6 Servings

HANDS-ON TIME: 10 Minutes

COOKING TIME: 30 Minutes

TOTAL TIME: 50 Minutes

BUTTONS TO USE: Pressure Cook

RELEASE TYPE: Natural Release

A 6–7 pound (2.75–3.25 kg) turkey—the perfect size for an intimate dinner party—will easily fit in your six-quart multicooker, and it will produce the juiciest, most tender turkey your guests have ever had. To give the turkey a beautiful golden-brown finish, pop it under the broiler for about five minutes. And if you're more in the mood for chicken, this recipes works great for a whole 7-pound (3.25 kg) chicken, as well.

Rinse the turkey and remove the giblets from the cavity. Pat the bird dry, and then rub the olive oil underneath the breast skin.

Sprinkle the entire turkey with the seasoned salt, paprika, and pepper. Fill the cavity of the turkey with the lime and half of the onion.

Pour the chicken broth into the Instant Pot inner pot. Place the turkey into the pot, breast side up. Place the remaining onion, rosemary, and thyme on top of and around the turkey.

Secure the lid, ensuring the valve is turned to the Sealing position. Press the Pressure Cook button and set the time to 30 minutes.

continued

1 (6–7-pound) (2.75–3.25 kg) young turkey or a 7-pound whole chicken

1 tablespoon olive oil

1 tablespoon seasoned salt

1 tablespoon smoked paprika

1 teaspoon pepper

1 lime, quartered

1 medium onion, peeled and quartered

1 cup (240 ml) chicken broth

2 sprigs fresh rosemary

4 sprigs fresh thyme

2 tablespoons butter, softened

When cooking is complete, let the pot sit for another 20 minutes, and then turn the valve to the Venting position to release any remaining pressure. Turn on the oven broiler.

Remove the lid and carefully transfer the turkey from the pot to a broiling pan, breast side up. Lightly pat the turkey dry with paper towels. Spread the softened butter over the turkey and place it under the broiler, breast up, and approximately 5 inches (12.5 cm) below the heat source.

Leave the turkey under the broiler for approximately 5 minutes, and check it, occasionally, to make sure that the skin does not burn. Remove the turkey when skin has turned a deep golden-brown color.

Let the turkey rest 5–10 minutes before carving.

TIP: When you are browning the turkey under the broiler, rotate it frequently to ensure even browning. Also, be sure to save the turkey carcass to make Turkey Bone Broth (page 145).

BEEF POT ROAST

YIELD: 6 Servings
HANDS-ON TIME: 5 Minutes
COOKING TIME: 60 Minutes
TOTAL TIME: 90 Minutes
BUTTONS TO USE: Pressure Cook
RELEASE TYPE: Natural Release

Jalapeño peppers add just the right amount of heat to this tender pot roast. Even your guests who don't like "spicy" will love it! In this recipe, the carrots and onions become quite soft, as they cook in the pot with the meat, but if you want them to be firmer, you can always toss the vegetables into the pot, after the cooking process is done, and let them cook for another five minutes.

Add all the ingredients, except the cilantro, to the Instant Pot inner pot. Secure the lid, ensuring the valve is turned to the Sealing position. Press the Meat/Stew button and set the time to 60 minutes.

When cooking is complete, let the pot sit for another 15 minutes, and then turn the valve to the Venting position to release any remaining pressure.

Remove the lid and lightly stir the ingredients. Break up the beef into large chunks and remove any excess fat. Transfer the meat and vegetables to a serving platter and garnish the dish with additional fresh jalapeño peppers and the fresh cilantro leaves. Season with salt and pepper, to taste.

1 (5–6-pound) (2.25–2.75 kg) beef chuck roast

1 (1-ounce) (30 g) package dry onion soup mix

1 (16-ounce) (475 ml) jar pearl (cocktail) onions, drained

3 large carrots, peeled and cut into 3–4-inch (8–10 cm) pieces

2 jalapeños, sliced (remove seeds if less heat is desired)

4 cloves garlic, peeled and smashed

1 teaspoon salt

½ teaspoon pepper

1 cup (240 ml) beef broth

fresh cilantro leaves for garnish

COLORFUL
VEGGIE LASAGNA

YIELD: 6 Servings

HANDS-ON TIME: 15 Minutes

COOKING TIME: 20 Minutes

TOTAL TIME: 50 Minutes

BUTTONS TO USE: Pressure Cook

RELEASE TYPE: Natural Release

Thanks to the Instant Pot and oven-ready lasagna noodles, you can have this fresh and colorful vegetable lasagna ready for your veggie loving guests in less than one hour. Don't be surprised if they skip some of the more traditional dishes just to get a bite of this one. You'll need a 7-inch (18 cm) springform pan for this dish. (See "Pot-in-Pot Cooking Method" on page xiv.)

In a large bowl, mix together the squash, zucchini, onion, spinach, green bell pepper, red bell pepper, salt, and pepper. Set the bowl aside.

In a medium bowl, mix together the ricotta cheese, egg, and Italian seasoning until the ingredients are well blended.

Break the lasagna noodles into 2–3-inch (5–8 cm) pieces or wedges.

Spray the springform pan with cooking spray. Pour ½ cup (120 ml) of the marinara sauce into the pan and spread it evenly over the bottom. Top the sauce with one-third of the broken lasagna noodles. It is okay if the noodles overlap.

Top the lasagna noodles with 2 cups (480 g) of the veggie mix, pressing down on the mixture in order to fit as much of it as possible in the pan. Top the veggie layer with one-third of the ricotta mixture, spreading it into a thin layer. Repeat the layering process until the pan is full.

1 small yellow squash, diced

1 small green zucchini, diced

½ small white onion, diced

4 ounces (115 g) baby spinach

1 small green bell pepper, seeded and thinly sliced

1 small red bell pepper, seeded and thinly sliced

1 teaspoon salt

½ teaspoon pepper

15 ounces (425 g) ricotta cheese

1 large egg

1 teaspoon Italian seasoning

6 ounces (170 g) oven-ready noodles (½ of a 12-ounce [340 g] package)

cooking spray

2 cups (480 ml) marinara sauce

1 cup (120 g) shredded mozzarella cheese

½ cup (45 g) Parmesan cheese

Place mozzarella and Parmesan on top of the mixture in the pan while gently pressing down to compact all the ingredients. Cover the pan with foil.

Place the Instant Pot steam rack in the Instant Pot inner pot and add 1 cup (240 ml) of water. Place the lasagna onto the steam rack.

Secure the lid, ensuring the valve is turned to the Sealing position. Set the time to 20 minutes.

When cooking is complete, let the pot sit for another 10 minutes, and then turn the valve to the Venting position to release any remaining pressure.

Carefully remove the lasagna and take off the foil. If you like, place the lasagna under the broiler to brown the cheese. Let the lasagna rest for 5 minutes before serving.

NOTE: The ingredient list calls for more vegetables than you will use in this recipe (it's a little hard to buy half of a squash or a zucchini), but you can always use the leftovers in a salad.

EASY
DUCK À L'ORANGE

YIELD: 4 Servings

HANDS-ON TIME: 10 Minutes

COOKING TIME: 12 Minutes

TOTAL TIME: 40 Minutes

BUTTONS TO USE: Sauté and Pressure Cook

RELEASE TYPE: Natural Release

Luscious, sweet, and tangy orange sauce served over crispy, tender duck will please even the most discerning dinner guest. While it's tempting to save this dish for only special occasions, it is such a snap to make that it could easily become a weeknight favorite.

4 duck thigh quarters, bone-in

1 teaspoon salt

½ teaspoon pepper

1 tablespoon vegetable oil

1 cup (240 ml) chicken broth

1 cup (240 ml) orange juice

½ (100 g) cup sugar

zest from one orange

1 tablespoon Grand Marnier® (optional)

2 tablespoons cornstarch mixed with 2 tablespoons water, for slurry

thin orange slices for garnish

Trim any excess skin from the duck quarters. Sprinkle the meat, on all sides, with salt and pepper.

Press the Sauté button to heat the Instant Pot inner pot. When the display reads "Hot," add the 1 tablespoon of vegetable oil to coat the bottom. Place the duck pieces skin side down into the hot pot in a single layer. If the pieces are large, you may have to cook them in two batches. Sear each side of the meat until it is until golden brown, approximately 4 minutes per side.

Remove the duck from the pot in order to deglaze the pot. Add the chicken broth to the pot and scrape the bottom with a wooden spoon, making sure to scrape up all the brown bits.

Add the orange juice and sugar to the pot, stirring constantly, until the sugar is dissolved, about 2 minutes. Add the orange zest and stir the pot. Press Cancel to turn off the sauté function.

continued

Place the duck pieces back into pot, skin side up. Secure the lid, ensuring the valve is turned to the Sealing position. Press the Pressure Cook button and set the time to 12 minutes.

When cooking is complete, let the pot sit for another 10 minutes, and then turn the valve to the Venting position to release any remaining pressure. Turn on the broiler while the pressure is releasing.

Remove the lid when all the pressure has released. Using tongs, transfer the duck pieces from the pot to a broiler pan. Place the pan under the broiler until the duck skin becomes crispy, after 5–10 minutes.

While the duck is under the broiler, press the Sauté button and add in the Grand Marnier (if using) and the cornstarch and water slurry, whisking the sauce constantly until it has thickened. Press Cancel to turn off the sauté function.

Remove the duck from the oven, place it on a serving platter, and spoon the sauce over the top. Garnish the duck with thin slices of orange.

TIP: Duck can also be served medium-rare. Simply reduce the cooking time by 4 minutes.

BEEF STROGANOFF

YIELD: 4 Servings

HANDS-ON TIME: 10 Minutes

COOKING TIME: 2 Minutes

TOTAL TIME: 20 Minutes

BUTTONS TO USE: Sauté and Pressure Cook

RELEASE TYPE: Natural Release

This easy-to-make, super-fast recipe can be made in one pot and in 20 minutes, and yet it yields a sublime dish that is elegant enough to serve to even your most sophisticated guests.

Press the Sauté button to heat the Instant Pot inner pot. When the display reads, "Hot," add the butter. When the butter is melted, add the shallots. Sauté the shallots for 3 minutes, and then add the garlic. Sauté the mixture for 1 minute more.

Add the beef to the pot and sear the strips on both sides, approximately 30 seconds per side. Remove the beef and place it in a bowl. It will not be fully cooked at this point.

Add the mushrooms, thyme, tarragon, and salt to the pot and stir the mixture until the mushrooms just begin to release their juices, about 4 minutes. Return the beef and any juices in the bowl back to the pot.

Press Cancel to turn off the sauté function. Add the noodles and broth to the pot. Stir the mixture to combine it well. Secure the lid, ensuring the valve is turned to the Sealing position. Press the Pressure Cook button and set the time to 2 minutes.

When cooking is complete, let the pot sit for another 5 minutes, and then turn the valve to the Venting position to release any remaining pressure. Remove the lid, stir the mixture, and stir in the sour cream. Garnish with the sliced green onions.

4 tablespoons butter

2 large shallots, minced

2 cloves garlic, minced

1½ pounds (68 g) sirloin, cut into thin strips

1 pound (450 g) sliced mushrooms

½ teaspoon dried thyme

½ teaspoon dried tarragon

2 teaspoons salt

1 pound extra wide egg noodles

3 cups (720 ml) beef broth

1 cup (240 g) sour cream, room temperature

sliced green onions for garnish

BEER-BRAISED SHREDDED BEEF

YIELD: 6 Servings

HANDS-ON TIME: 10 Minutes

COOKING TIME: 60 Minutes

TOTAL TIME: 90 Minutes

BUTTONS TO USE: Sauté and Meat/Stew

RELEASE TYPE: Natural Release

A heaping platter of tender shredded beef is a great go-to for casual, buffet-style get-togethers. Serve it with warm, sliced rolls.

2 tablespoons olive oil

1 (5–6-pound) (2.25–2.75 kg) beef chuck roast, trimmed and cut into 4–5-inch (10–13 cm) pieces

1 medium onion, sliced

5 cloves garlic, peeled and smashed

1 (12-ounce) (330 ml) bottle dark beer

1 teaspoon salt

1 teaspoon pepper

1 lime cut into wedges for garnish

cilantro leaves for garnish

dinner rolls for serving

Press the Sauté button to heat the Instant Pot inner pot. When the display reads "Hot," add the oil to coat the bottom of the pot. To sear the pieces of beef, let them sit undisturbed in the pot for 3 minutes. Turn over the pieces and let them sear on the other side 2 more minutes.

When all the beef is browned, add the onion, garlic, beer, salt, and pepper. (Make sure all the beef is in the pot.) Stir the mixture well, making sure to scrape the bottom of the pot with a wooden spoon to remove any brown bits. Secure the lid, ensuring the valve is turned to the Sealing position. Press the Meat/Stew button and set the time to 60 minutes.

When cooking is complete, let the pot sit for another 20 minutes, and then turn the valve toward the Venting position to release any remaining pressure.

Remove the lid and transfer the beef chunks and onion to a serving platter, using tongs. Shred the beef and remove any large pieces of fat. Squeeze the lime juice from the wedges on top of the beef and place a few additional lime wedges on and around the beef, for garnish. Top the dish with the cilantro and serve it with sliced dinner rolls.

TIP: Depending on the size of your Instant Pot, you might need to brown the beef in batches in order to not overcrowd the pot. If so, repeat the cooking process for the second batch.

STEAMED LOBSTER TAILS

YIELD: 2 Servings

HANDS-ON TIME: 2 Minutes

COOKING TIME: 2 Minutes

TOTAL TIME: 7 Minutes

BUTTONS TO USE: Pressure Cook

RELEASE TYPE: Quick Release

This is undoubtedly one of the dishes that have prompted some to nickname the Instant Pot the "miracle pot." The bright and vibrant lobster tails in this recipe, which are served with lemon butter dipping sauce, are good enough to rival even the best seafood restaurant. And the ingredients go from frozen to picture perfect in less than ten minutes. Truly amazing.

2 (4-ounce) (110 g) lobster tails, frozen (or use thawed or fresh lobster tails—both will work)

4 tablespoons butter, melted

1 tablespoon lemon juice

Position the Instant Pot steam rack in the Instant Pot inner pot and add 1 cup (240 ml) of water. Place the frozen lobster tails side by side on top of the steam rack. Secure the lid, ensuring the valve is turned to the Sealing position. Set the time to 2 minutes.

When cooking is complete, turn the valve to the Venting position to release the pressure. Remove the lid and, using tongs, transfer the lobster tails to a serving plate.

Using kitchen shears, cut the top of the lobster shell lengthwise down the middle.

Whisk together the melted butter and lemon juice in a small bowl. Drizzle the butter and lemon sauce over the top of the lobster or serve it in a small dish, on the side, for dipping.

ROAST PORK LOIN

YIELD: 6 Servings

HANDS-ON TIME: 10 Minutes

COOKING TIME: 20 Minutes

TOTAL TIME: 45 Minutes

BUTTONS TO USE: Sauté and Pressure Cook

RELEASE TYPE: Natural Release

To make this dish into an easy but festive weeknight dinner, top the pork with a generous scoop of Apple–Orange Chutney (page 77) and a sprinkling of fresh pomegranate seeds.

1 (2–3-pound) (900 g–1.3 kg) pork loin

1 teaspoon salt

1 teaspoon pepper

2 tablespoons butter

1 cup (240 ml) apple juice

1 large onion, sliced into 1-inch (3 cm) pieces

Apple-Orange Chutney (page 77), optional

fresh pomegranate seeds for garnish, optional

Liberally season all sides of the pork roast with salt and pepper. Select the Sauté button to heat up the Instant Pot inner pot.

When the display reads "Hot," add the butter to the pot. As soon as the butter melts, add the pork roast to the pot and sear it on all sides, approximately 4 minutes per side.

Add the apple juice to the pot and use a wooden spoon to scrape up any brown bits from the bottom of the pot. Add the onion. Press Cancel to turn off the sauté function.

Secure the lid, ensuring the valve is turned to the Sealing position. Press the Pressure Cook button and set the time to 20 minutes.

When cooking is complete, let the pot sit for another 15 minutes, and then turn the valve to the Venting position to release any remaining pressure.

Remove the lid and transfer the pork to a cutting board. Let the pork rest for 5 minutes, and then cut it into ¾-inch (2 cm) slices. Top the pork roast with chutney and fresh pomegranate seeds, if using.

VENISON ROAST

YIELD: 6 Servings

HANDS-ON TIME: 10 Minutes

COOKING TIME: 70 Minutes

TOTAL TIME: 100 Minutes (plus marinating overnight)

BUTTONS TO USE: Sauté and Pressure Cook

RELEASE TYPE: Natural Release

There's no better time to serve venison than at a holiday gathering. With a little bit of prep and the wonders of the Instant Pot, it will likely be the best your family has ever tasted.

Trim as much fat as possible off the roast. Put the meat in a zip top bag and add the buttermilk. Seal the bag and let it sit in the refrigerator overnight. This step is very important because it helps to remove some of the gamey taste from the venison.

When you are ready to cook the venison, remove it from the buttermilk and wipe off any excess buttermilk.

Press the Sauté button repeatedly until the display indicates "High" to heat the Instant Pot inner pot. When the display reads "Hot," add the butter to the pot. As soon as the butter has melted, sear the venison roast on all sides by letting it sit undisturbed in the pot for approximately 5 minutes per side.

Press Cancel to stop the sauté function. Add 1 cup (240 ml) of water and scrape up all the brown bits from the bottom of the pot with a wooden spoon. It may be easier to do this if you temporarily remove the roast from the pot. Once all the bits have been scraped up from the pot, put the roast back into the pot.

2–3-pound (900 g–1.3 kg) venison roast (also called venison ham roast)

2 cups (480 ml) buttermilk for marinating the venison overnight

4 tablespoons butter

1 (1-ounce) (28 g) packet of powdered brown gravy mix

1 medium onion, cut into 1-inch (3 cm) slices

salt and pepper to taste

lime wedges for garnish

warm bread, for serving

Sprinkle the roast with the powdered gravy mix and add the onion slices. Secure the lid, ensuring the valve is turned to the Sealing position. Press the Meat/Stew button and set the time to 70 minutes.

When cooking is complete, let the pot sit for another 15 minutes, and then turn the valve to the Venting position to release any remaining pressure. Remove the lid and transfer the roast to a large serving platter. Shred the meat into large chunks, using two forks, and remove any remaining fat. Sprinkle the roast liberally with salt and pepper. Add a squeeze of lime juice and garnish the roast with lime wedges, if desired. Serve the venison with warm bread.

TURKEY BREAST
FOR TWO

If all you need is just enough turkey for two (with some left-over), this is your dish. It's quick, easy to make, and the turkey is especially moist and flavorful when you brine the meat. The steps are easy and the results are worth it!

YIELD: 2 Servings
HANDS-ON TIME: 5 Minutes
COOKING TIME: 20 Minutes
TOTAL TIME: 30 Minutes (plus brining)
BUTTONS TO USE: Pressure Cook
RELEASE TYPE: Natural Release

FOR THE BRINE

¼ cup (50 g) salt

¼ cup (50 g) sugar

1 (2–3-pound) (900 g–1.3 kg) bone-in turkey breast

FOR THE TURKEY

1 medium onion, peeled and quartered

2 cloves garlic, peeled and smashed

1 cup (240 ml) apple juice

1 tablespoon butter, softened

salt and pepper to taste

parsley for garnish

TO BRINE THE TURKEY

Place the salt, sugar, and 2 cups (480 ml) of water in a 1-gallon (3.75 liter) zip top bag. Close the bag and vigorously shake it to combine the ingredients. Add the turkey breast to the bag. Press as much air out of the bag as possible and seal it. Refrigerate the bag for 1–2 hours.

TO COOK THE TURKEY

Remove the turkey breast from the bag of brine. Rinse and pat it dry.

Place the turkey breast, onion, garlic, and apple juice in the Instant Pot inner pot. Secure the lid, ensuring the valve is turned to the Sealing position and press the Pressure Cook button. Set the time to 20 minutes.

When cooking is complete, let the pot sit for another 10 minutes. Turn the valve to the Venting position to release any remaining pressure. Turn on the oven broiler.

Remove the lid and transfer the turkey breast to a broiling pan, skin side up. Spread the softened butter on the turkey skin. Sprinkle the turkey breast with salt and pepper and place it under the broiler for 5–10 minutes, until the skin is golden and crisp.

Remove the broiler pan from the oven, transfer the turkey to a platter, and garnish it with the parsley.

PULLED PORK

YIELD: 6 Servings

HANDS-ON TIME: 10 Minutes

COOKING TIME: 60 Minutes

TOTAL TIME: 100 Minutes

BUTTONS TO USE: Meat/Stew

RELEASE TYPE: Natural Release

A big part of enjoying the holidays is getting the gang together for various sporting events to yell and scream at the referees and root for the home team. Pulled pork to the rescue! Serve a heaping platter of this fork-tender meat with soft dinner rolls buffet-style. Just make sure you're first in line.

Season the pork with the salt, pepper, and cumin.

Place the pork, onion, garlic, and apple juice into the Instant Pot inner pot and briefly stir the mixture to combine it. Secure the lid, ensuring the valve is turned to the Sealing position. Press the Meat/Stew button and set the time to 60 minutes.

When cooking is complete, let the pot sit for another 20 minutes, and then turn the valve to the Venting position to release any remaining pressure.

Remove the lid and transfer the pork to a serving platter. Remove any remaining pieces of fat. Sprinkle the pork with additional salt and pepper, to taste. Garnish the pork with the lime wedges and cilantro.

TIP: If you'd like to give some of the pork a bit of crispiness, place the pork on a rimmed baking sheet and pop it under the broiler for 5–10 minutes.

5–6-pound (2.25–2.75 kg) boneless pork shoulder (also called pork butt), large pieces of fat removed and cut into 4–5-inch (10–13 cm) pieces

2 tablespoons salt

2 tablespoons pepper

1 tablespoon ground cumin

1 medium onion, peeled and cut into wedges

4 garlic cloves, peeled and smashed

2 cups (480 ml) apple juice

lime wedges for garnish

cilantro, chopped, for garnish

SOUS VIDE
FILET MIGNON

YIELD: 4 Filets

HANDS-ON TIME: 10 Minutes

COOKING TIME: 90 Minutes

TOTAL TIME: 100 Minutes

APPLIANCE TO USE: Instant Pot
Accu Slim Sous Vide
Immersion Circulator

RELEASE TYPE: None

If you're hankering for the perfect, melt-in-your-mouth steak, sous vide is exactly the right method to use. This much-celebrated French cooking technique, which is now readily accessible to everyone, thanks to the Instant Pot Accu Slim Sous Vide Immersion Circulator, is especially kind to meat, by cooking every part of it at exactly the same temperature. The results are nothing short of miraculous. To give the filet mignon a gorgeous crust, finish them in a hot cast iron skillet or on a grill for 15 seconds per side. (See page xv for more details about using the sous vide immersion circulator.)

4 (8-ounce) (225 g) filet mignon steaks

2 tablespoons olive oil

½ teaspoon salt

½ teaspoon pepper

4 garlic cloves, peeled and smashed

4 sprigs fresh rosemary

2 tablespoons butter

1 teaspoon high smoke point oil, such as grape seed oil

rosemary for serving

Drizzle the olive oil over the filets on both sides and sprinkle them with the salt and pepper. Place 1 of the smashed garlic cloves and 1 sprig of rosemary on top of each filet, and then place each of the filets into an airtight, sealed bag. Use vacuum-sealed food bags or heavy-duty zip top bags, removing as much air as possible from the bags before sealing them.

If you like, refrigerate the filets, in their individual airtight bags, overnight, to let them absorb more flavor, or you can cook them immediately.

continued

Fill the Instant Pot inner pot (or other large pot) ¾ full with water. Insert the Sous Vide cooker, secure it to the side, and select the desired temperature and time. (A temperature of 129°F [54°C] for 90 minutes is perfect for a medium-rare 1–2-inch [2.5 to 5 cm] filet.) Wait for the water to heat to the desired temperature.

Place the sealed steaks in the pot of water, ensuring that they are fully submerged. It may be necessary to weigh them down with a heatproof plate on top, or clip each bag to the side of the pot so the steaks are fully submerged.

When cooking is complete, remove the bags, cut them open, and remove the steaks. Pat them dry and discard the garlic and rosemary.

Heat a cast iron skillet (or grill) over high heat. Add the butter and grape seed oil to the pan. When the butter has melted, place the steaks in the pan. Sear each side for 15 seconds and then promptly remove the steak to prevent overcooking. Season with additional salt and pepper, to taste, and serve the steaks immediately with fresh rosemary.

SOUS VIDE
SEARED TUNA

YIELD: 4 Filets

HANDS-ON TIME: 10 Minutes

COOKING TIME: 45 Minutes

TOTAL TIME: 60 Minutes

BUTTONS TO USE: Instant Pot
Accu Slim Sous Vide
Immersion Circulator

RELEASE TYPE: None

You never have to worry about overcooking tuna filets again! With just a little advance planning, you can use the Instant Pot Accu Slim Sous Vide Immersion Circulator to make perfect filets. To give the fish a nice crust, finish the filets in a hot cast iron skillet for 15 seconds per side. (See page xv for more details about using the sous vide immersion circulator.) Serve with sticky rice, if you like.

4 (6-ounce) (170 g)
fresh tuna filets

2 tablespoons olive oil

½ teaspoon salt

½ teaspoon pepper

2 medium shallots, thinly sliced

4 sprigs fresh thyme

2 tablespoons sesame seeds,
optional, for crust

2 tablespoons vegetable oil

Drizzle the olive oil over both sides of the filets and sprinkle them with the salt and pepper. Place 1 of the smashed garlic cloves and 1 sprig of thyme on top of each filet, and then place each of the filets into an airtight, sealed bag. Use vacuum-sealed food bags or heavy-duty zip top bags, removing as much air as possible from the bags before sealing them.

Let the filets rest for 30 minutes in the refrigerator.

Fill the Instant Pot inner pot (or other large pot) ¾ full with water. Insert the Sous Vide cooker, secure it to the side, and select the desired temperature and time (115°F [46°C] for 45 minutes is perfect for a medium-rare 1–2-inch [3–5 cm] filet.). Wait for the water to heat to the desired temperature.

Place the sealed filets in the pot of water, ensuring that they are fully submerged. It may be necessary to weigh them down with a heatproof plate on top, or clip each bag to the side of the pot so that they are fully submerged. When cooking is complete, remove the bags, cut them open, and remove the tuna. Pat the fish dry and discard the garlic and thyme. Season the fish with additional salt and pepper, to taste, and, if you like, sprinkle the filets with the sesame seeds.

Heat a cast iron skillet over high heat. Add the oil to the pan. When the oil starts to shimmer, place the tuna in the pan. Sear each side for 15 seconds and then promptly remove the fish from the pan to prevent overcooking.

Spectacular
SIDES, SAUCES & DRESSINGS

Acorn Squash
with Shallots & Grapes 55

Chunky Cinnamon
Applesauce 56

Sweet Potatoes &
Marshmallows 57

White Beans with
Bacon & Rosemary 58

Savory Pumpkin Risotto 61

Cauliflower Au Gratin 62

Nutmeg Spaghetti
Squash 63

Leek, Parsnip & Herb
Brioche Dressing 64

Pomegranate
Brussels Sprouts 66

Winter Vegetable Mix 68

Mushroom Medley 69

Sausage & Sage Stuffing 71

Classic Mashed Potatoes 73

Easy Herb Gravy 74

Green Beans
with Toasted Almonds 75

Apple-Orange Chutney 77

Fresh Cranberry Sauce 78

Steamed Baby Potatoes
with Shallots 79

The Best Beet Salad 81

No-Soak Black Beans
with Ginger & Nutmeg 83

ACORN SQUASH WITH SHALLOTS & GRAPES

YIELD: 4 Servings
HANDS-ON TIME: 5 Minutes
COOKING TIME: 4 Minutes
TOTAL TIME: 25 Minutes
BUTTONS TO USE: Pressure Cook
RELEASE TYPE: Natural Release

At your next holiday dinner, dress up the table with tender squash loaded with flavorful grapes, shallots, and a touch of sage, a combination that will delight your guests and keep them talking about the meal for months to come.

2 small acorn squash, cut in half lengthwise, seeds removed

2 tablespoons olive oil

1 tablespoon fresh sage, chopped

½ teaspoon salt

½ teaspoon pepper

1 pound (450 g) red grapes (approximately 40 grapes)

2 medium shallots, peeled and sliced crosswise into thin slices.

salt and pepper to taste

Drizzle ½ tablespoon of the olive oil over each half of the acorn squash. Sprinkle the squash with the sage and the salt and pepper. Place about 10 grapes into each of the cavities in the squash, then sprinkle the grapes with the shallot slices.

Position the Instant Pot steam rack in the Instant Pot inner pot and add 1 cup (240 ml) of water. Carefully place each of the squash halves onto the steam rack, with the cavity side up. It's okay if the squash overlaps slightly to fit in the pot.

Secure the lid, ensuring the valve is turned to the Sealing position. Press the Pressure Cook button and set the time to 4 minutes.

When cooking is complete, let the pot sit undisturbed for 10 minutes, and then turn the valve to the Venting position. When the pressure has released, remove the lid and carefully lift the squash out of the pot, using tongs. Season the squash with additional salt and pepper to taste. Serve immediately.

TIP: If the squash halves are too big to fit side by side in one layer on the steam rack, carefully stand each of the squash halves at a 30-degree angle, and lean them against the sides of the inner pot.

CHUNKY CINNAMON APPLESAUCE

YIELD: 4 Cups (1 kg)

HANDS-ON TIME: 10 Minutes

COOKING TIME: 8 Minutes

TOTAL TIME: 30 Minutes

BUTTONS TO USE: Pressure Cook

RELEASE TYPE: Natural Release

Fresh, homemade applesauce with a hint of cinnamon, a splash of lemon juice, and just the right amount of chunkiness makes the perfect accompaniment to almost any roast, especially the Roast Pork Loin (page 41).

Place the apples, sugar, lemon juice, cinnamon, nutmeg, and salt into the Instant Pot inner pot. Add ½ cup (240 ml) of water and stir.

Secure the lid, ensuring the valve is turned to the Sealing position. Press the Pressure Cook button and set the time to 8 minutes.

When cooking is complete, let the pot sit undisturbed for 10 minutes, and then turn the valve to the Venting position. When all the pressure has released, remove the lid and stir the contents of the pot until the applesauce reaches the desired consistency. Stir the sauce with a fork for a chunkier texture. Use an immersion blender for a very smooth texture.

TIP: For sweeter applesauce, increase the amount of sugar to ¼ cup (50 g).

10 apples (½ Granny Smith and ½ Gala or any other combination of tart and sweet apples), peeled, cored, and quartered

2 tablespoons sugar

2 teaspoons fresh lemon juice

½ teaspoon ground cinnamon

¼ teaspoon nutmeg

pinch salt

½ cup (120 ml) water

SWEET POTATOES & MARSHMALLOWS

YIELD: 8 Servings

HANDS-ON TIME: 10 Minutes

COOKING TIME: 3 Minutes

TOTAL TIME: 15 Minutes

BUTTONS TO USE: Pressure Cook

RELEASE TYPE: Quick Release

These perfectly soft sweet potatoes (you can also use yams) mixed with just the right amount of marshmallows, cinnamon, nutmeg, and butter will have your guests asking for seconds before they finish the first serving. They're that good.

Place the sweet potatoes, brown sugar, cinnamon salt, and nutmeg into the Instant Pot inner pot. Stir the mixture to combine it.

Add 1½ cups (75 g) of the marshmallows to the pot and stir them into the sweet potato mixture. Places the pieces of butter on top of the mixture. Add ¾ cup (180 ml) water.

Secure the lid, ensuring the valve is turned to the Sealing position. Press the Pressure Cook button and set the time to 3 minutes.

When cooking is complete, carefully turn the valve to the Venting position to release the pressure. Remove the lid and gently stir the sweet potato mixture to combine all the ingredients. Transfer the mixture to a serving dish and top it with the remaining ½ cup (25 g) of the mini marshmallows.

TIP: If you would like to toast the marshmallows on top of the sweet potatoes, transfer the mixture to an oven-safe dish, add an additional 1 cup (50 g) of mini marshmallows, and place the dish under the broiler for 3–5 minutes until the top turns golden brown.

5 pounds (2.25 kg) red-colored sweet potatoes (or yams), peeled and cut into 4-inch chunks

1 cup (200 g) brown sugar

1 teaspoon cinnamon

½ teaspoon salt

¼ teaspoon nutmeg

2 cups (100 g) mini marshmallows, divided

4 tablespoons butter, cut into ½-inch (1 cm) pieces

WHITE BEANS WITH BACON & ROSEMARY

YIELD: 8 Servings
HANDS-ON TIME: 10 Minutes
COOKING TIME: 25 Minutes
TOTAL TIME: 60 Minutes
BUTTONS TO USE: Sauté and Pressure Cook
RELEASE TYPE: Natural Release

Rosemary and sage add a little touch of magic to creamy white beans. Top this hearty dish with some crispy bacon, and it will quickly become a family favorite, particularly in the fall and winter, when everyone can use a dose of soul-satisfying comfort food.

(12-ounce [340 g] package) bacon, sliced crosswise into ½-inch (1 cm) pieces

1 pound (450 g) dry white beans (cannellini beans), rinsed

3 sprigs fresh rosemary plus extra for garnish

2 dried bay leaves

6 sage leaves, chopped

2 gloves garlic, peeled and smashed

1 teaspoon salt

Press the Sauté button to heat up the Instant Pot inner pot. When the display reads "Hot," add the bacon pieces and sauté them for about 7 minutes, or until the bacon is crisp. Stir the bacon occasionally while it cooks. Press Cancel to turn off the Sauté function. Remove the bacon from the pot with a slotted spoon and transfer it to a paper towel–lined plate. Reserve the bacon.

Pour the bacon fat out of the pot and into a small measuring cup. Reserve 2 tablespoons of the fat for later use. Wipe the inside of the pot clean.

Add the beans, rosemary sprigs, bay leaves, sage, garlic, salt, and 6 cups (1.5 liters) of water to the pot. Add the 2 tablespoons of reserved bacon fat. Stir the mixture well.

Secure the lid, ensuring the valve is turned to the Sealing position. Press the Pressure Cook button and set the time to 25 minutes.

When cooking is complete, let the pot sit for another 10 minutes, and then carefully turn the valve to the Venting position to release any remaining pressure. Remove the lid when the pressure has released.

Using a slotted spoon, remove the beans from the pot and place them in a serving dish. Discard the sprigs of rosemary and any of the large rosemary leaves, as well as the bay leaves. Top the beans with the reserved pieces of crispy bacon and garnish the dish with some fresh rosemary sprigs. Season the beans with additional salt and pepper, to taste.

SAVORY PUMPKIN RISOTTO

YIELD: 6 Servings

HANDS-ON TIME: 10 Minutes

COOKING TIME: 6 Minutes

TOTAL TIME: 20 Minutes

BUTTONS TO USE: Sauté and Pressure Cook

RELEASE TYPE: Quick Release

No babysitting is required for this pumpkiny riff on classic risotto. Gone are the days of standing over a hot stove while constantly stirring rice. Your guests will never know just how easy it is to make this perfect risotto!

2 tablespoons butter

2 shallots, minced

2 cloves of garlic, minced

2 cups (360 g) short grain rice (Arborio)

¼ cup (60 ml) dry white wine

4 cups (950 ml) vegetable (or chicken) broth

1 (15-ounce) (425 g) can pumpkin puree

¼ cup (20 g) fresh, grated Parmesan cheese and extra for serving

Press the Sauté button to heat up the Instant Pot inner pot. When the display reads "Hot," add the butter. Add the shallots to the pot and sauté them for 3–4 minutes. Add the garlic and sauté the mixture for 1 minute more.

Add the rice and stir it into the mixture until the rice is well coated. Slowly stir the wine into the rice mixture until most of it has been absorbed. Press the Cancel button to turn off the sauté function.

Add the broth to the pot, stir the mixture, and secure the lid, ensuring the valve is turned to the Sealing position. Press the Pressure Cook button and set the time to 6 minutes.

When cooking is complete, turn the valve to the Venting position to release the pressure. Remove the lid when all the pressure is released.

Add the pumpkin purée and stir it into the rice mixture until it is well combined.

Add the Parmesan cheese and give the mixture a good stir. Serve the risotto hot with freshly grated cheese.

CAULIFLOWER AU GRATIN

YIELD: 6 Servings
HANDS-ON TIME: 5 Minutes
COOKING TIME: 2 Minutes
TOTAL TIME: 10 Minutes
BUTTONS TO USE: Pressure Cook
RELEASE TYPE: Quick Release

Goat cheese and heavy cream transform everyday cauliflower into a to-die-for side dish. To make this rich gratin, you will need a 7-inch-wide (18 cm) ovenproof baking dish. (See "Pot-in-Pot Cooking Method" on page xiv.)

1 large head cauliflower, cut into 2-inch (5 cm) florets

1 cup (240 ml) heavy cream

4 ounces (115 g) goat cheese, cut into pieces

2 tablespoons butter, cut into small pieces

½ teaspoon salt

¼ teaspoon pepper

1 cup (85 g) grated Parmesan cheese

freshly grated nutmeg for garnish, optional

Place the cauliflower florets into the baking dish. Pour the cream over the top and place the pieces of goat cheese and butter on top of and around the cauliflower.

Sprinkle cauliflower with salt and pepper, and top it with the Parmesan cheese.

Cover the baking dish with aluminum foil.

Place the Instant Pot steam rack into the Instant Pot inner pot and add 1 cup (240 ml) of water.

Place the baking dish on top of the steam rack. Secure the lid, ensuring the valve is turned to the Sealing position. Press the Pressure Cook button and set the time to 2 minutes.

When cooking is complete, turn the valve to the Venting position to release the pressure. Remove the lid and carefully lift the baking dish out of the pot, using oven mitts.

Remove the foil and gently stir the mixture to combine the cauliflower and cheeses. Sprinkle the freshly grated nutmeg over the top, if you like, and serve.

NUTMEG SPAGHETTI SQUASH

YIELD: 4 Servings
HANDS-ON TIME: 5 Minutes
COOKING TIME: 7 Minutes
TOTAL TIME: 15 Minutes
BUTTONS TO USE: Pressure Cook
RELEASE TYPE: Quick Release

This fun and interesting side dish is a great alternative to pasta. Use a microplane to grate fresh nutmeg over the top of the squash, just before putting it on the table. The aroma is heavenly.

½ cup (120 ml) white wine

1 fresh spaghetti squash, 6–8 inches (15–20 cm) long, cut in half and seeded

¼ teaspoon freshly grated nutmeg

salt and pepper to taste

Place the Instant Pot steam rack into the Instant Pot inner pot. Pour the wine and ¼ cup (60 ml) of water under the steam rack. Set the spaghetti squash halves on top of the steam rack, standing them on end, if necessary, to fit the pot.

Secure the lid, ensuring the valve is turned to the Sealing position. Press the Pressure Cook button and set the time to 7 minutes.

When cooking is complete, turn the valve to the Venting position to release the pressure. Remove the lid and lift out the squash, using tongs.

Place the squash on a plate, flesh side up. With a fork, scrape the flesh from the shell toward the center to create long, thin strands of "spaghetti." Sprinkle the squash with the freshly grated nutmeg and season with salt and pepper to taste. Serve piping hot.

LEEK, PARSNIP & HERB BRIOCHE DRESSING

YIELD: 6 Servings

HANDS-ON TIME: 10 Minutes

COOKING TIME: 20 Minutes

TOTAL TIME: 45 Minutes

BUTTONS TO USE: Sauté and Pressure Cook

RELEASE TYPE: Quick Release

If you're looking for a unique side dish that everyone will love, try this recipe, with its warm and toasty chunks of brioche loaded with parsnip tidbits, sautéed leeks, and fresh thyme. You will need a 7-inch (18 cm) springform pan or a 1-quart (1 liter) ovenproof dish that fits in your Instant Pot inner pot to make this recipe. (See "Pot-in-Pot Cooking Method" on page xiv.)

12-ounce (350 g) loaf, brioche bread, cut into 1- to 2-inch (3–5 cm) chunks

3 eggs

½ cup (120 ml) heavy cream

½ teaspoon salt

½ teaspoon pepper

3 tablespoons butter

1 large leek, white parts sliced in half and then crosswise into ½-inch (1 cm) strips

½ pound (225 g) parsnips, peeled and diced into ½-inch (1 cm) pieces

1 tablespoon fresh thyme leaves

½ cup (45 g) fresh, shredded Parmesan cheese

cooking spray

Place the chunks of brioche into a large bowl. Set it aside.

In a small bowl, mix the eggs, cream, and the salt and pepper until the mixture is well combined.

Press the Sauté button to heat up the Instant Pot inner pot. When the display reads "Hot," add the butter. When the butter has melted, add the leek and parsnips, and sauté them for about 5 minutes, until they have just turned soft. Add the thyme and mix it in well. Press the Cancel button to turn off the sauté function.

Add the egg mixture to the chunks of brioche and gently combine it with the bread until it is evenly coated. Add the parsnip mixture and stir it gently into the brioche mix. Fold in the Parmesan cheese. Rinse out the Instant Pot inner pot.

Spray the springform pan with cooking spray. Spoon the bread mixture into the pan and spread it evenly over the bottom. Cover the pan with foil.

Position the Instant Pot steam rack in the clean Instant Pot inner pot and add 1 cup (240 ml) of water.

Place the covered springform pan on top of the steam rack. Secure the lid, ensuring the valve is turned to the Sealing position. Press the Pressure Cook button and set the time to 30 minutes. Toward the end of the cooking cycle turn on the oven broiler.

After 30 minutes, turn the valve to the Venting position to release the pressure. Carefully remove the lid and lift out the springform pan, using oven mitts.

Remove the foil and place the springform pan under the broiler for about 5 minutes, until the brioche is crisp and golden on top.

Remove the pan from the oven and let it sit for 5 minutes. Remove the outer ring of the springform pan and slide the brioche dressing onto a serving plate using a spatula. Serve it warm.

POMEGRANATE BRUSSELS SPROUTS

YIELD: 6 Servings

HANDS-ON TIME: 5 Minutes

COOKING TIME: 0 Minutes

TOTAL TIME: 15 Minutes

BUTTONS TO USE: Sauté and Pressure Cook

RELEASE TYPE: Quick Release

These tender Brussels sprouts tossed in a maple glaze and topped with bright red pomegranate seeds and a sprinkling of hazelnuts will add a blast of color to your holiday table.

Press the Sauté button to heat the Instant Pot inner pot. When the display reads "Hot," add the butter. As soon as the butter has melted, add the Brussels sprouts to the pot and sear them, cut side down, for about 1 minute. Give the sprouts a stir, add the broth, and scrape up any brown bits on the bottom of the pot with a wooden spoon.

Press the Cancel button to turn off the sauté function. Secure the lid, ensuring the valve is turned to the Sealing position. Press the Pressure Cook button and set the time to 0 (zero).

As soon as the pressure has built up and the display reads "0," immediately turn the valve to the Venting position to release the pressure. Remove the lid and, using a slotted spoon, immediately transfer the Brussels sprouts to a serving dish.

To make the glaze, whisk together the maple syrup and cider vinegar in a small bowl. Drizzle the glaze over the Brussels sprouts and gently toss them to evenly coat the sprouts with the glaze.

Sprinkle the pomegranate seeds, hazelnuts, and the salt and pepper over the Brussels sprouts and serve them immediately.

2 tablespoons butter

1½ pounds (675 g) medium-size Brussels sprouts, trimmed and cut in half lengthwise

¾ cup (180 ml) vegetable or chicken broth

2 tablespoons maple syrup

2 tablespoons apple cider vinegar

1 cup (155 g) fresh pomegranate seeds

½ cup (75 g) hazelnuts

½ teaspoon salt

¼ teaspoon pepper

TIP: The key to success with Brussels sprouts is to not overcook them; make sure to remove them from the Instant Pot as soon as the cooking cycle is complete and pressure is released.

WINTER VEGETABLE MIX

YIELD: 6 Servings

HANDS-ON TIME: 10 Minutes

COOKING TIME: 2 Minutes

TOTAL TIME: 15 Minutes

BUTTONS TO USE: Steam

RELEASE TYPE: Quick Release

All the best winter vegetables are brought together in this heart-healthy, warm, and comforting dish. To make it, you will need a steamer basket that fits in your Instant Pot.

In a large bowl, mix together all the vegetables, the Italian seasoning, and the salt and pepper.

Position the steamer basket into the Instant Pot inner pot and add 1 cup (240 ml) of water. Place the vegetable mix in the steamer basket. Secure the lid, ensuring the valve is turned to the Sealing position.

Press the Steam button and set the time to 2 minutes.

When cooking is complete, turn the valve to the Venting position to release the pressure. Remove the lid and immediately transfer the vegetables to a serving platter. Drizzle the vegetables with melted butter, if using, and season them with additional salt and pepper to taste.

TIP: If you prefer your veggies more al dente, reduce the cooking time to 1 minute.

2 medium carrots, peeled and cut into 2–3-inch (5–8 cm) pieces, about 2 cups (480 ml)

2 medium parsnips, peeled and cut into 2–3-inch (5–8 cm) pieces, about 2 cups (480 ml)

2 cups (280 g) cauliflower florets

2 cups (230 g) baby potatoes, skin on and quartered into 1–2-inch (3–5 cm) pieces

2 leeks, white parts only, rinsed and cut once lengthwise, then crosswise into 1-inch (3 cm) strips

1 teaspoon Italian seasoning

1 teaspoon salt

½ teaspoon pepper

1 tablespoon melted butter, optional

MUSHROOM MEDLEY

YIELD: 6 Servings

HANDS-ON TIME: 5 Minutes

COOKING TIME: 3 Minutes

TOTAL TIME: 10 Minutes

BUTTONS TO USE: Pressure Cook

RELEASE TYPE: Quick Release

Rich and earthy mushrooms are a great addition to any holiday plate. This dish includes a wonderful mix of many different kinds of mushrooms, but feel free to use your favorites instead, if you like.

Place all the ingredients, except the parsley, in the Instant Pot inner pot. Stir the mixture to combine the ingredients. Secure the lid, ensuring the valve is turned to the Sealing position. Press the Pressure Cook button and set the time to 3 minutes.

When cooking is complete, turn the valve to the Venting position to release the pressure. Remove the lid and give the mixture a good stir. Use a slotted spoon to transfer the mushrooms to a serving dish. Sprinkle the parsley over the top of the mushrooms and serve them immediately.

1 large sweet onion, halved and sliced into ½-inch (1 cm) strips

8 ounces (225 g) cremini mushrooms, sliced

8 ounces (225 g) white button mushrooms, sliced

3 ounces (85 g) oyster mushrooms, sliced

3 ounces (85 g) shitake mushrooms, sliced

2 tablespoons butter

1 clove garlic, minced

¾ cup (180 ml) vegetable or beef broth

chopped parsley for garnish

SAUSAGE & SAGE STUFFING

YIELD: 6 Servings

HANDS-ON TIME: 15 Minutes

COOKING TIME: 20 Minutes

TOTAL TIME: 45 Minutes

BUTTONS TO USE: Sauté and Pressure Cook

RELEASE TYPE: Quick Release

Every traditional holiday flavor comes through in this delicious herby stuffing, but be warned: it's so good, you probably won't have any leftovers. To make the stuffing, you will need a 7-inch (18 cm) springform pan or a 1-quart (1 liter) ovenproof baking dish that fits your Instant Pot. (See "Pot-in-Pot Cooking Method" on page xiv.)

4 tablespoons butter

1 medium onion, minced

3 celery stalks, finely chopped

3 gloves garlic, minced

1 pound (450 g) ground Italian sausage, sweet or hot

4 cups (360 g) dried bread cubes, either store-bought stuffing cubes or bread, cut into 1-inch (3 cm) pieces and air-dried on a cookie sheet overnight

¼ cup (8 g) minced fresh sage (or 2 teaspoons dried sage)

1½ cups (360 ml) vegetable or chicken broth

2 eggs, lightly beaten

½ teaspoon salt

½ teaspoon pepper

cooking spray

chopped parsley for garnish

Press the Sauté button to heat up the Instant Pot inner pot. When the display reads "Hot," add the butter. As soon as the butter melts, add the onion, celery, and garlic. Sauté the veggies for 3 minutes, and then add the sausage. Break up the sausage into small crumbles with a wooden spoon and continue to brown the sausage until it is no longer pink. Press Cancel to turn off the Sauté function.

In a large bowl, mix together the dried bread cubes, sausage mixture, sage, broth, eggs, and the salt and pepper. Gently mix until the bread is well coated. Let the mixture sit for 2 minutes until the bread has absorbed the liquid.

Spray the springform pan or baking dish with cooking spray.

Scoop the bread and sausage mixture into the springform pan, pressing it down, if necessary, to fit it all in the pan. Cover the pan with foil.

continued

Clean the inner pot, and then place back into the Instant Pot. Put the Instant Pot steam rack into the inner pot and add 1 cup (240 ml) of water. Place the springform pan onto the steam rack. Secure the lid, ensuring the valve is turned to the Sealing position. Press Pressure Cook and set the time to 20 minutes.

When cooking is complete, turn the valve to the Venting position to release the pressure. Remove the lid.

Turn on the oven broiler.

Remove the springform pan from the Instant Pot and remove the foil covering. Place the springform pan under the broiler for about 5 minutes, until the stuffing is lightly golden.

Remove the stuffing from the oven, garnish it with the parsley, and let the pan sit for 5 minutes before serving.

CLASSIC MASHED POTATOES

YIELD: 6 Servings

HANDS-ON TIME: 10 Minutes

COOKING TIME: 7 Minutes

TOTAL TIME: 30 Minutes

BUTTONS TO USE: Pressure Cook

RELEASE TYPE: Natural Release

A touch of butter and sour cream, whipped or beaten into soft, cooked russet potatoes, results in perfectly consistent, creamy mashed potatoes every time.

Place the potatoes, salt, and ¾ cup (180 ml) of water into the Instant Pot inner pot. Secure the lid, ensuring the valve is turned to the Sealing position. Press the Pressure Cook button and set the time to 7 minutes.

When cooking is complete, let the pot sit for another 10 minutes, and then turn the valve to the Venting position to release any additional pressure.

Remove the lid, and add the butter and sour cream. Use a potato masher or handheld blender to mash the potatoes until they are very smooth potatoes. Add salt, to taste.

Serve the potatoes warm with an extra pat of butter, if desired.

3 pounds (1.3 kg) russet potatoes, peeled and cut into 3-inch (8 cm) chunks

2 teaspoons salt

6 tablespoons butter, cut into pieces

1 cup (240 g) sour cream

EASY HERB GRAVY

YIELD: 4 Cups (950 ml)

HANDS-ON TIME: 5 Minutes

COOKING TIME: 20 Minutes

TOTAL TIME: 30 Minutes

BUTTONS TO USE: Pressure Cook and Sauté

RELEASE TYPE: Quick Release

No giblets are required for this creamy, flavorful gravy, which goes perfectly with turkey. The recipe works every time and can easily be doubled for the gravy lovers in your family.

Add the broth, thyme, rosemary, sage, and the salt and pepper to the Instant Pot inner pot. Secure the lid, ensuring the valve is turned to the Sealing position. Press the Pressure Cook button and set the time to 20 minutes.

When cooking is complete, turn the valve to the Venting position to release the pressure. Remove the lid.

Press the Sauté button. When the gravy begins to lightly simmer, whisk in the butter and stir it in, until it has completely melted. Add the slurry to the gravy, whisking constantly until the desired thickness has been reached. Press Cancel to turn off the pot. Taste the gravy and add additional salt and pepper as needed. Transfer the gravy to a serving dish and serve it piping hot.

4 cups (950 ml) chicken (or turkey) broth

1 tablespoon fresh thyme leaves

1 tablespoon fresh rosemary leaves, finely chopped

1 tablespoon fresh sage, finely chopped

½ teaspoon salt

½ teaspoon pepper

4 tablespoons butter

2 tablespoons cornstarch mixed with 2 tablespoons water, for slurry

GREEN BEANS WITH TOASTED ALMONDS

YIELD: 6 Servings
HANDS-ON TIME: 5 Minutes
COOKING TIME: 2 Minutes
TOTAL TIME: 10 Minutes
BUTTONS TO USE: Steam
RELEASE TYPE: Quick Release

Toasted, slivered almonds add a touch of crunch to these fresh, vibrant green beans. A squeeze of lemon gives them a nice, bright finish. You will need a steamer basket that fits in your Instant Pot to prepare this dish.

2 pounds (905 g) fresh green beans, ends trimmed

1 teaspoon fresh lemon juice

1 tablespoon (pat) butter

½ teaspoon salt

¼ cup (28 g) slivered almonds, lightly toasted in a dry skillet

Position the steamer basket in the Instant Pot inner pot and add 1 cup (240 ml) of water. Place the green beans in the steamer basket and secure the lid, ensuring the valve is turned to the Sealing position. Press the Steam button and set the time to 2 minutes.

When cooking is complete, immediately turn the valve to the Venting position to release the pressure. Remove the lid and use tongs to transfer the beans from the pot to a serving platter.

Top the beans with the butter and a sprinkle of salt and toasted almonds. Serve immediately.

TIP: If you prefer crispy green beans, reduce the cooking time to 1 minute.

APPLE-ORANGE CHUTNEY

YIELD: 4 Cups (950 ml)
HANDS-ON TIME: 10 Minutes
COOKING TIME: 10 Minutes
TOTAL TIME: 25 Minutes
BUTTONS TO USE: Pressure Cook
RELEASE TYPE: Quick Release

This savory and sweet blend of apples, orange juice, ginger, and a sprinkle of red pepper flakes brightens up any pork dish. Try it with the Roast Pork Loin (page 41).

Place all the ingredients in the Instant Pot inner pot and combine them with a good stir. Secure the lid, ensuring the valve is turned to the Sealing position. Press the Pressure Cook button and set the time to 10 minutes.

When cooking is complete, turn the valve to the Venting position to release the pressure. Remove the lid, stir, and serve the chutney either hot or cold.

8 Granny Smith apples, peeled, cored, and cut into 2-inch (5 cm) pieces

1 cup (85 g) raisins

½ medium white onion, diced

2 tablespoons fresh ginger, minced

1 cup (240 ml) orange juice

½ cup (120 ml) apple cider vinegar

½ cup (100 g) brown sugar

1 teaspoon salt

¼ teaspoon red pepper flakes

¼ teaspoon ground nutmeg

FRESH CRANBERRY SAUCE

YIELD: 2 Cups (480 ml)
HANDS-ON TIME: 5 Minutes
COOKING TIME: 2 Minutes
TOTAL TIME: 10 Minutes
BUTTONS TO USE: Pressure Cook
RELEASE TYPE: Quick Release

Nothing compliments holiday meals better than a bright, fresh, and tart cranberry sauce, served either hot or cold.

4 cups (400 g) fresh cranberries
½ cup (100 g) sugar

Place the cranberries and sugar in the Instant Pot inner pot along with 1 cup (240 ml) of water. Secure the lid, ensuring the valve is turned to the Sealing position. Press the Pressure Cook button and set the time to 2 minutes.

When cooking is complete, turn the valve to the Venting position to release the pressure. Remove the lid and stir the mixture. The sauce will thicken as it is stirred. Transfer the cranberry sauce to a serving bowl.

STEAMED BABY POTATOES WITH SHALLOTS

YIELD: 6 Servings
HANDS-ON TIME: 5 Minutes
COOKING TIME: 7 Minutes
TOTAL TIME: 15 Minutes
BUTTONS TO USE: Steam
RELEASE TYPE: Quick Release

Baby golden potatoes steamed to perfection—and with hints of shallots and rosemary—have long been a favorite on holiday tables. To make these tender potatoes, you will need a steamer basket that fits in your Instant Pot.

3 pounds (1.3 kg) Yukon Gold or other baby yellow potatoes, approximately 1–2 inches (3–5 cm) in diameter

1 large shallot, thinly sliced

1 tablespoon fresh rosemary, finely minced (or 1 teaspoon dried rosemary)

1 tablespoon butter

½ teaspoon salt

¼ teaspoon pepper

chopped parsley for garnish

Position the steamer basket in the Instant Pot inner pot and add 1 cup (240 ml) of water. Place the potatoes in the steamer basket and sprinkle them with the slices of shallot and rosemary.

Secure the lid, ensuring the valve is turned to the Sealing position. Press the Steam button and set the time to 7 minutes.

When cooking is complete, turn the valve to the Venting position to release the pressure. Remove the lid and transfer the potatoes to a serving dish.

Add the butter and the salt and pepper to the potato-shallot mixture and stir it well to coat the potatoes. Sprinkle the chopped parsley over the potatoes as a garnish, and serve them warm.

THE BEST
BEET SALAD

YIELD: 6 Servings
HANDS-ON TIME: 10 Minutes
COOKING TIME: 15 Minutes
TOTAL TIME: 30 Minutes
BUTTONS TO USE: Pressure Cook
RELEASE TYPE: Quick Release

Making a beet salad, like this colorful, uber-healthy version, used to take hours, but now you can make it in minutes and enjoy it any time. Thin slices of fennel add crunch and extra freshness to the mix.

TO PREPARE THE BEETS

Remove the leafy green stalks and roots from the beets, being careful not to cut the skin. Do not peel the beets.

Position the Instant Pot steam rack in the Instant Pot inner pot and add 1 cup (240 ml) of water. Place the beets on top of the steam rack. Secure the lid, ensuring the valve is turned to the Sealing position. Select Pressure Cook and set the time to 15 minutes.

When cooking is complete, turn the valve to the Venting position to release the pressure. Remove the lid and, using tongs, lift the beets out of the pot.

Let the beets cool for 5–10 minutes. When the beets are cool enough to handle, run them under cool water in the sink. Using a paper towel, scrub the skin off the beets under the running water.

Cut the clean beets into 1–2-inch (3–5 cm) pieces.

FOR THE BEETS

8–10 medium or large beets

FOR THE DRESSING

3 tablespoons honey

3 tablespoons balsamic vinegar

½ teaspoon salt

¼ teaspoon pepper

FOR THE SALAD

2 cups (75 g) lettuce of choice, chopped

1 large shallot, minced

1 bulb fennel, thinly sliced

½ cup (55 g) walnut pieces

4 ounces (115 g) crumbled blue cheese

fennel fronds, for garnish (if desired)

continued

TO PREPARE THE DRESSING

In a small bowl, whisk together the honey, balsamic vinegar, salt, and pepper. Set the bowl aside.

TO PREPARE THE SALAD

Spread the lettuce on a serving platter and top the greens with the beets, shallots, fennel, walnuts, and blue cheese. Drizzle the dressing over the top and serve the beets warm or cold. Garnish with fennel fronds, if desired.

TIP: Beets can temporarily stain your hands and countertops, so use gloves when you handle them, and promptly wipe down any surfaces that come in contact with beet juice.

NO-SOAK BLACK BEANS WITH GINGER & NUTMEG

YIELD: 6 Servings

HANDS-ON TIME: 5 Minutes

COOKING TIME: 30 Minutes

TOTAL TIME: 45 Minutes

BUTTONS TO USE: Bean/Chili

RELEASE TYPE: Natural Release

This recipe is an example of one of the many things that your Instant Pot does best. Here it transforms dry beans into plump, tender, flavorful beans. No soaking required!

Place all the ingredients, except the parsley, in the Instant Pot inner pot. Add 6 cups (1.5 liters) of water and stir. Secure the lid, ensuring the valve is turned to the Sealing position. Press the Bean/Chili button and set the time to 30 minutes.

When cooking is complete, let the pot sit for another 15 minutes, and then turn the valve to the Venting position to release any remaining pressure.

Remove the lid, stir the beans, and transfer them to a serving platter, using a slotted spoon. Remove the bay leaf. Top the beans with a dusting of freshly grated nutmeg and some finely chopped Italian parsley.

1 pound (450 g) dry black beans, rinsed well

1 tablespoon minced fresh ginger

½ teaspoon fresh, grated nutmeg, plus more for additional garnish

1 bay leaf

1 tablespoon vegetable oil

1 teaspoon salt

Italian parsley, finely chopped

A Happy Ending
DESSERTS

Upside Down, Nutty,
Pull-Apart Cinnamon
Rolls 87

Warm Cherries Jubilee 89

Super-Moist Pumpkin Pie
Spice Cake 90

Super-Simple Chocolate
Mint Brownies 93

Berry Cobbler with
Granola Topping 95

Creamy Cheesecake
with a Touch of Orange 96

Lemon Curd Tart 99

Seasonal Rice Pudding 101

Stuffed Cinnamon
Walnut Apples 103

Red Velvet Cheesecake 104

Spiced Apple Crisp 106

Warm Fruit & Nut
Compote 107

Baileys Lava Cakes 109

Christmas Fudge 111

Pumpkin Cream Lava
Cake 112

UPSIDE DOWN, NUTTY, PULL-APART CINNAMON ROLLS

YIELD: 6 Servings
HANDS-ON TIME: 5 Minutes
COOKING TIME: 20 Minutes
TOTAL TIME: 40 Minutes
BUTTONS TO USE: Pressure Cook
RELEASE TYPE: Quick Release

This dessert is a delicious, sticky hybrid that combines everything you love about cinnamon rolls and bread pudding. Set a platter of this gooey, cinnamony goodness on the dessert table at your next holiday get-together and watch it disappear! And if your dessert table is already full, this also makes an amazing holiday morning breakfast meal. You will need a round 7-inch (18 cm) springform pan or ovenproof baking dish to make this recipe. (See "Pot-in-Pot Cooking Method" on page xiv.)

Cut the cinnamon rolls into quarters.

Place the sugar and cinnamon in a gallon-size zip top bag and shake it to combine the sugar and cinnamon. Add the quartered cinnamon rolls to bag, seal the top, and shake the bag vigorously to coat all the pieces.

Spray the springform pan or baking dish with cooking spray. If you're using a springform pan, wrap two layers of aluminum foil around the bottom of the pan to prevent any leakage.

Place the cinnamon roll pieces in the springform pan or baking dish in one layer.

FOR THE ROLLS

1 (17½-ounce) (495 g) can refrigerated cinnamon rolls (either with or without icing)

¼ cup (50 g) sugar

1 tablespoon cinnamon

cooking spray

4 tablespoons butter

¼ cup (60 ml) milk

½ cup (60 g) chopped pecans, divided

FOR THE ICING

1 cup (120 g) powdered sugar

3 tablespoons milk

options: use the icing included with the cinnamon rolls

continued

Add the butter and milk to a small saucepan and place the pan over low heat until the butter melts. (Or use a microwave on 50% power for 1 minute.)

Drizzle the butter and milk combination over the pieces of cinnamon roll.

Position the steam rack in the Instant Pot inner pot and add 1 cup (240 ml) of water. Place the springform pan or baking dish on top of the steam rack. Secure the lid, ensuring the valve is turned to the Sealing position. Press the Pressure Cook button and set the time to 20 minutes.

While the cinnamon roll is cooking, turn on the broiler.

When cooking is complete, carefully turn the valve to the Venting position to release the pressure. Remove the lid.

Sprinkle ¼ cup (30 g) of the pecans on top of the cinnamon roll, and then carefully remove the springform pan from the pot. Place the pan under the broiler for about 5 minutes, until the top is slightly golden.

Remove the pan from the oven and let sit for 10 minutes. Slide a knife along the inside edge of the springform pan to release the cinnamon roll from pan. Remove the ring of springform pan.

To invert the cinnamon roll, place a large plate on top of the roll, and then turn the pan upside down. Slide a spatula or knife beneath the bottom of the springform pan (which should now be on top) to release the cinnamon roll onto the plate.

If making icing, in a small bowl, whisk together the powdered sugar and milk until well-blended. Drizzle the top of the inverted cinnamon roll with the icing or use the packaged icing. Sprinkle remaining pecans on top of the cinnamon roll and serve it warm.

WARM CHERRIES JUBILEE

YIELD: 6 Servings

HANDS-ON TIME: 5 Minutes

COOKING TIME: 1 Minute

TOTAL TIME: 10 Minutes

BUTTONS TO USE: Pressure Cook

RELEASE TYPE: Quick Release

You can serve this tangy, classy dessert when you have only ten minutes to spare, because that's all you'll need to get this time-tested classic on the table for your guests. Add a glug of brandy, after the cooking process, for an extra layer of warmth. The cherries can be served on their own, or over a scoop of vanilla ice cream.

2 (15-ounce) (425 g) cans whole, tart cherries, packed in water

2 tablespoons sugar

1 teaspoon lemon juice

2 tablespoons cornstarch mixed with 2 tablespoons water, for the slurry

¼ cup (60 ml) brandy (optional)

Place the cherries (including the water from the can), sugar, and lemon juice in the Instant Pot inner pot. Combine all the ingredients with a good stir. Secure the lid, ensuring the valve is turned to the Sealing position. Press Pressure Cook and set the time to 1 minute.

When cooking is complete, turn the valve to the Venting position to release the pressure.

Open the lid and press Cancel to turn the pot off, and then press Sauté. Add the brandy, if you like (it's optional), and then add the slurry. Stir the mixture for about 1 minute, until is turns thick. Press Cancel as soon as the desired thickness is reached.

Serve the cherries by themselves or spoon them over ice cream. Delicious!

SUPER-MOIST PUMPKIN PIE SPICE CAKE

YIELD: 8 Servings

HANDS-ON TIME: 15 Minutes

COOKING TIME: 20 Minutes

TOTAL TIME: 50 Minutes

BUTTONS TO USE: Pressure Cook

RELEASE TYPE: Quick Release

The hints of cinnamon, nutmeg, and pumpkin leave no doubt that this flavorful, dense cake is perfect for fall and winter holiday tables, and who can resist cream cheese frosting? You will need a round 7-inch (18 cm) springform pan or ovenproof baking dish for this recipe. (See "Pot-in-Pot Cooking Method" on page xiv.)

TO PREPARE THE CAKE

In a large bowl, using a hand blender, mix together the oil and the eggs, and then mix in both sugars until the ingredients are well blended. Add the pumpkin puree and vanilla to the mix and blend it until it is smooth.

In a medium bowl, whisk together the flour, baking powder, pumpkin pie spice, cinnamon, and salt.

Slowly add the dry ingredient mixture to the egg mixture and blend the ingredients together with a spatula until they're just mixed. Do not overmix.

Spray the springform pan with the cooking spray, and then pour the batter into the pan. Cover the pan with aluminum foil.

FOR THE CAKE

1 cup (240 ml) vegetable oil

4 large eggs, room temperature

1 cup (200 g) brown sugar

½ cup (100 g) sugar

1 (15-ounce)(425 g) can pumpkin puree

1 teaspoon vanilla

2 cups (240 g) flour

2 ½ teaspoons baking powder

2 teaspoons pumpkin pie spice

1 teaspoon ground cinnamon

½ teaspoon salt

cooking spray

FOR THE FROSTING

8 ounces (225 g) cream cheese, room temperature

½ cup (115 g) butter, room temperature

2 cups (240 g) powdered sugar

1 teaspoon vanilla extract

Position the Instant Pot steam rack in the Instant Pot inner pot and add 1 cup (240 ml) of water. Place the springform pan on top of the steam rack. Secure the lid, ensuring the valve is turned to the Sealing position. Press the Pressure Cook button and set the time to 25 minutes.

When cooking is complete, turn the valve to the Venting position to release the pressure.

Remove the lid and lift the springform pan out of the pot, using oven mitts. Set the pan on a cooling rack and allow the cake to cool. Run a small knife along the inside of the springform pan to release the cake from the sides. Remove rim of the springform pan.

Using a thin spatula remove the cake from the bottom of the springform pan and transfer it to a serving platter.

TO PREPARE THE FROSTING

In a medium-size bowl, mix the cream cheese and butter with a hand blender, until they are well mixed. Add the powdered sugar to the bowl, one cup at a time, and blend it into the mixture until it is smooth. Add the vanilla and blend until it is well incorporated.

Using a small spatula spread the frosting over the top of the cake, slice into 8 pieces, and serve at room temperature.

SUPER-SIMPLE CHOCOLATE MINT BROWNIES

YIELD: 12 Brownies
HANDS-ON TIME: 15 Minutes
COOKING TIME: 30 Minutes
TOTAL TIME: 50 Minutes
BUTTONS TO USE: Pressure Cook
RELEASE TYPE: Quick Release

If you're enjoying these rich, minty brownies at the end of an evening meal, pair them with a glass of good red wine. It's a surprisingly delicious combo. You will need a 7-inch (18 cm) springform pan for this recipe. (See "Pot-in-Pot Cooking Method" on page xiv.)

Spray the inside of the springform pan with the cooking spray. Set the pan aside.

In a large bowl mix together the melted butter, cocoa powder, sugar, flour, and salt until the mixture is well blended. Add the vanilla, peppermint extract (if using), and eggs and mix until well combined. Fold in the mint chocolate chips.

Pour the batter into the springform pan.

Position the Instant Pot steam rack in the Instant Pot inner pot and add 1 cup (240 ml) of water. Place the batter-filled springform pan on top of the steam rack.

Secure the lid, ensuring the valve is turned to the Sealing position. Press the Pressure Cook button and set the time to 30 minutes.

continued

cooking spray

8 tablespoons (115 g) butter, melted

1 cup (80 g) cocoa powder

1 cup (200 g) sugar

⅔ cup (85 g) flour

pinch of salt

½ teaspoon vanilla extract

½ teaspoon peppermint extract (optional)

2 large eggs

1 cup (200 g) mint chocolate chips

When cooking is complete, turn the valve to the Venting position to release the pressure. Remove the lid.

Remove the springform pan and blot the top of the brownie dry with a paper towel, if necessary. Cool the brownie on a wire rack for at least 10 minutes. Remove the rim and then the bottom of the springform pan, and transfer the brownies to a serving plate. Cut the brownie into 12 bite-size squares to serve.

TIP: For the peanut butter lover in your family, try this variation. Just eliminate the peppermint extract and substitute 1 cup (200 g) of peanut butter chips in place of the mint chocolate chips and follow the directions as written.

BERRY COBBLER WITH GRANOLA TOPPING

YIELD: 6 Servings

HANDS-ON TIME: 5 Minutes

COOKING TIME: 5 Minutes

TOTAL TIME: 15 Minutes

BUTTONS TO USE: Pressure Cook

RELEASE TYPE: Quick Release

Tart blackberries and tangy blueberries come together beautifully here to form a rich, syrupy dessert that's topped with crunchy granola. To make this delicious (not to mention antioxidant-rich) treat, you will need a 2-quart (2-liter) heatproof baking dish that can fit in your Instant Pot. (See "Pot-in-Pot Cooking Method" on page xiv.)

1 (16-ounce) (450 g) package frozen blackberries (or 2 cups [285 g] fresh blackberries)

1 (12-ounce) (340 g) package frozen blueberries (or 2 cups [290 g] fresh blueberries)

½ cup (100 g) sugar

¼ teaspoon ground cinnamon

½ teaspoon fresh lemon zest

2 cups (250 g) crunchy granola of choice

In a large bowl, mix together all the ingredients, except the granola. Pour the mixture into the baking dish. Top it with the granola and cover the dish with aluminum foil.

Position the Instant Pot steam rack in the Instant Pot inner pot and add 1 cup (240 ml) of water. Place the baking dish on top of the steam rack. Secure the lid, ensuring the valve it is turned to the Sealing position. Press the Pressure Cook button and set the time to 5 minutes.

When cooking is complete, turn the valve to the Venting position to release the pressure. Remove the lid.

Lift the baking dish out of the pot with oven mitts and remove the aluminum foil. Serve the cobbler immediately or place under the broiler for 5 minutes to crisp the granola. The cobbler is delicious served with ice cream or a dollop of whipped cream.

CREAMY CHEESECAKE WITH A TOUCH OF ORANGE

YIELD: 8 Servings

HANDS-ON TIME: 15 Minutes

COOKING TIME: 30 Minutes

TOTAL TIME: 60 Minutes

BUTTONS TO USE: Pressure Cook

RELEASE TYPE: Natural Release

It is no secret that the Instant Pot makes an amazing cheesecake. The hint of orange in this recipe brightens up the whole cake. You will need a 7-inch (18 cm) springform pan for this recipe. (See "Pot-in-Pot Cooking Method" on page xiv.)

TO PREPARE THE CRUST

Spray the springform pan with the cooking spray. Set the pan aside.

In a medium bowl, combine the graham cracker crumbs, the melted butter, and the sugar. Spoon the crust mixture into the springform pan.

Press the crust down with a flat object, such as the bottom of a small glass, allowing the mixture to come about ½ inch (1 cm) up the sides of the pan. Place the prepared springform pan in the freezer while you prepare the filling.

TO PREPARE THE FILLING

In a large bowl, blend together the cream cheese, sour cream, and vanilla with a hand mixer on medium-low speed. In a separate small bowl, mix together the sugar and cornstarch.

FOR THE CRUST

cooking spray

2 cups (170 g)
graham cracker crumbs

6 tablespoons (85 g) butter, melted

½ cup (100 g) sugar

FOR THE FILLING

16 ounces (450 g) cream cheese, at room temperature

½ cup (120 g) sour cream

1½ teaspoons vanilla

½ cup (100 g) sugar

2 tablespoons cornstarch

1½ teaspoons freshly grated orange zest

2 large eggs, at room temperature

4–6 thin orange slices for the topping

Add half of the sugar mixture to the cream cheese mixture and blend it until it is smooth. Add the remaining sugar mixture to the bowl and blend it until it, too, is smooth. Add the orange zest to the mixture and beat it in until it is well blended. Add the eggs one at a time to the mixture and mix, using the hand mixer on medium speed. Blend until the eggs have been fully incorporated and the mixture is smooth.

Pour the filling into the prepared crust in the springform pan. Gently tap the pan against the counter to eliminate any trapped bubbles in the filling.

Position the Instant Pot steam rack in the Instant Pot inner pot and add 1 cup (240 g) of water. Cover the cheesecake with heavy-duty aluminum foil. Poke several holes in the foil so that it can vent. Place the springform pan on top of the steam rack.

Secure the lid, ensuring the valve is turned to the Sealing position. Press the Pressure Cook button and set the time to 30 minutes.

When cooking is complete, let the pot sit for another 15 minutes, and then turn the valve to the Venting position to release any additional pressure. Remove the lid.

Lift the springform pan out of the pot and let it cool at room temperature for 10 minutes. Run a small paring knife around the inner edges of the pan to release the crust. Carefully remove the springform pan rim and place the cheesecake in the refrigerator for at least 4 hours.

Run a knife between the crust and the bottom of the pan to release the cheesecake. Using a large, thin spatula, carefully transfer the cheesecake to a serving platter. Top it with the orange slices and serve.

LEMON CURD TART

YIELD: 12 Servings

HANDS-ON TIME: 10 Minutes

COOKING TIME: 5 Minutes

TOTAL TIME: 20 Minutes plus cooling time

BUTTONS TO USE: Pressure Cook

RELEASE TYPE: Natural Release

This tangy lemon tart is a refreshing alternative to heavier holiday desserts. You will need some prepared Lemon Curd (page 160) and a 7-inch (18 cm) springform pan for this recipe. (See "Pot-in-Pot Cooking Method" on page xiv.)

FOR THE CRUST

cooking spray

2 cups (170 g) graham cracker crumbs

6 tablespoons (85 g) butter, melted

½ cup (100 g) sugar

FOR THE FILLING

8 ounces (225 g) prepared Lemon Curd (page 160)

powdered sugar for topping, sifted

TO PREPARE THE CRUST

Spray the springform pan with the cooking spray. Set the pan aside.

In a medium bowl, combine the graham cracker crumbs, melted butter, and sugar. Spoon the mixture into the springform pan.

Press the crust down with a flat object, such as the bottom of a small glass, allowing the mixture to come about ½ inch (1 cm) up the sides of the pan. Place the prepared springform pan in the freezer while you prepare the filling.

TO PREPARE THE FILLING

Whisk the prepared lemon curd until it is smooth. Pour the lemon curd into the prepared graham cracker crust in the springform pan and smooth it with a spatula. Cover the pan with aluminum foil.

continued

Position the Instant Pot steam rack in the Instant Pot inner pot and add 1 cup (240 ml) of water. Place the springform pan on top of the steam rack. Secure the lid, ensuring the valve is turned to the Sealing position. Press the Pressure Cook button and set the time to 5 minutes.

When cooking is complete, turn the valve to the Venting position to release the pressure. Remove the lid and lift the springform pan from the pot, using oven mitts.

Place the springform pan on a cooling rack and let the lemon curd tart cool to room temperature. Slide a knife around the inside of the springform pan to release the tart. Remove the springform rim. Using a thin spatula to slide underneath the crust, carefully transfer the tart to a serving platter. Top with the sifted powdered sugar and slice into 12 wedges.

TIP: Short on time? You can buy a 7-ounce (200 g) jar of lemon curd and use it in this recipe.

SEASONAL RICE PUDDING

YIELD: 8 Servings

HANDS-ON TIME: 5 Minutes

COOKING TIME: 15 Minutes

TOTAL TIME: 30 Minutes

BUTTONS TO USE: Pressure Cook

RELEASE TYPE: Natural Release

Here, a dash of holiday spices elevates an everyday rice pudding to a wonderfully festive dish.

In a medium-size bowl, whisk the eggs. Add the milk and cream to the eggs and mix well.

Pour the milk mixture into the Instant Pot inner pot and add all the remaining ingredients. Stir them together thoroughly.

Secure the lid, ensuring that the valve is turned to the Sealing position. Press the Pressure Cook button and set the time to 15 minutes.

When cooking is complete, let the pot sit for another 5 minutes, and then turn the valve to the Venting position to release any remaining pressure.

Remove the lid and give the contents a good stir. The pudding will thicken as you stir it. Serve the rice pudding in individual dessert bowls and top them with additional raisins, if desired.

2 large eggs

4 cups (950 ml) whole milk

¾ cup (180 ml) heavy cream

1 cup (180 g) uncooked short grain white rice

1 cup (150 g) raisins

½ cup (100 g) brown sugar

1 ½ teaspoons vanilla

½ teaspoon ground cinnamon

½ teaspoon allspice

¼ teaspoon ground nutmeg

pinch of salt

STUFFED CINNAMON WALNUT APPLES

YIELD: 6 Servings

HANDS-ON TIME: 10 Minutes

COOKING TIME: 3 Minutes

TOTAL TIME: 15 Minutes

BUTTONS TO USE: Pressure Cook

RELEASE TYPE: Quick Release

The aroma of these warm, sweet apples stuffed with walnuts and raisins is the very essence of autumn and winter holiday fare.

6 medium honey crisp apples (or other good baking apples)

½ cup (60 g) crushed walnut pieces

½ cup (100 g) brown sugar

½ cup (85 g) golden (or regular) raisins

½ teaspoon ground cinnamon

¼ teaspoon ground nutmeg

1 cup (240 ml) apple juice

6 tablespoons (85 g) butter, cut into 6 pieces

Wash the apples and core them from the top using a melon-baller. Do not core all the way through the apple—leave about 1 inch (3 cm) intact on the bottom.

In a medium-size bowl, mix together the walnut pieces, brown sugar, raisins, cinnamon, and nutmeg. Fill the cavity of each apple with the walnut mixture.

Pour the apple juice into the Instant Pot inner pot. Place the apples, side by side, in a circle around the perimeter of the inner pot. Sprinkle any remaining walnut mixture (if there is any left over) on top of the apples. Top each apple with 1 tablespoon of the butter.

Secure the lid, ensuring the valve is turned to the Sealing position. Press the Pressure Cook button and set the time to 3 minutes.

When cooking is complete, turn the valve to the Venting position to release the pressure. Remove the lid.

Use tongs to carefully lift the apples out of the pot and a long-handled spoon to scoop out the juices. Place the apples in individual serving dishes and spoon the juices over the top.

RED VELVET CHEESECAKE

YIELD: 8 Servings

HANDS-ON TIME: 15 Minutes

COOKING TIME: 30 Minutes

TOTAL TIME: 60 Minutes

BUTTONS TO USE: Pressure Cook

RELEASE TYPE: Natural Release

It's easy to use your Instant Pot to create this popular cheese-cake. The dark chocolate crust and deep, rich, red velvety center of this amazing cheesecake will definitely win over the crowd, any time. To make the cheesecake, you will need a 7-inch (18 cm) springform pan. (See "Pot-in-Pot Cooking Method" on page xiv.)

TO PREPARE THE CRUST

Spray the springform pan with cooking spray.

Crush the Oreo cookies into fine crumbs, using a food processor.

In a medium-size bowl, mix together the cookie crumbs and melted butter, until they are well combined. The mixture should just barely hold together in a finger pinch.

Spoon the cookie crumb mixture into springform pan. Press the crust down with a flat object, such as the bottom of a small glass, allowing the mixture to come about ½ inch (1 cm) up the sides of the pan. Place the prepared springform pan in the freezer while you prepare the filling

FOR THE CRUST

cooking spray

2 cups crushed Oreo®
(or similar) cookies
(approximately half of a
14.3-ounce [500 g] package)

4 tablespoons butter, melted

FOR THE FILLING

16 ounces (450 g) cream cheese,
at room temperature

½ cup (43 g) sour cream

2 teaspoons vanilla

1 (1-ounce) (30 ml) bottle
red food coloring

2 tablespoons cornstarch

½ cup (100 g) sugar

¼ cup (20 g) cocoa powder

2 large eggs

pinch of salt

whipped cream for topping,
optional

TO PREPARE THE FILLING

In a medium-size bowl, blend together the cream cheese, sour cream, and vanilla with a hand mixer on medium-low speed until the mixture is smooth. Add the food coloring and blend it into the cream cheese mixture until it is fully incorporated.

In a separate small bowl mix cornstarch, sugar, and cocoa powder. Add half of the cornstarch mixture to the cream cheese mixture and blend it in well. Add the remaining half of the cornstarch mixture and blend it in until it is just combined. Add one egg at a time to the mixture and blend them in until they're just combined. Add a pinch of salt and stir to combine.

Pour the filling into the prepared springform pan. Firmly tap the pan against the counter to enable any trapped bubbles to rise to the top. Pierce any bubbles on top of the filling.

Position the Instant Pot steam rack in the Instant Pot inner pot. Add 1 cup (240 ml) of water. Carefully place the springform pan on top of the steam rack.

Secure the lid, ensuring the valve is turned to the Sealing position and press the Pressure Cook button. Set the time to 25 minutes.

When cooking is complete, let the pot sit for another 10 minutes, and then turn the valve to the Venting position to release any remaining pressure. Carefully remove the lid and take out the pan. Let it cool at room temperature for 10 minutes, and then run a small paring knife around the inner edge of the pan to release the crust. Remove the springform rim and place the cheesecake in the refrigerator to cool for at least 4 hours. Serve the cake with whipped cream if you'd like.

SPICED APPLE CRISP

YIELD: 6 Servings

HANDS-ON TIME: 10 Minutes

COOKING TIME: 3 Minutes

TOTAL TIME: 15 Minutes

BUTTONS TO USE: Pressure Cook

RELEASE TYPE: Quick Release

Make the most of apple season with this simple, warm fruit crisp topped with crunchy granola. Any baking apple will do, but a blend of sweet with tart apples gives a nice balance to the earthy spices in this dessert.

Place all the ingredients, except the granola, in the Instant Pot inner pot. Stir the mixture well. Secure the lid, ensuring that the valve is turned to the Sealing position. Press the Pressure Cook button and set the time to 3 minutes.

When cooking is complete, turn the valve to the Venting position to release the pressure. Remove the lid and stir the apples.

Using a slotted spoon, transfer the apples to individual dessert dishes and top them with the granola. Serve the crisp while it's warm.

10 baking medium-size apples (Granny Smith, Gala, Honey Crisp, or your choice of sweet and tart apples), peeled and sliced into 2-inch-thick (5 cm) slices

1 cup (150 g) golden raisins

½ cup (120 ml) apple cider

¼ cup (50 g) brown sugar

1 tablespoon honey

1 teaspoon cinnamon

½ teaspoon nutmeg

¼ teaspoon ground cloves

¼ teaspoon salt

2 cups (250 g) crunchy granola of your choice, for the topping

WARM FRUIT & NUT COMPOTE

YIELD: 6 Servings

HANDS-ON TIME: 10 Minutes

COOKING TIME: 1 Minutes

TOTAL TIME: 15 Minutes

BUTTONS TO USE: Pressure Cook

RELEASE TYPE: Quick Release

A medley of apples, blueberries, and fresh walnuts makes this a great option for a light dessert. Of course, no one can stop you from spooning it over a big bowl of ice cream.

Place all the ingredients except the walnuts in the Instant Pot inner pot. Add 1 cup (240 ml) water and stir well. Secure the lid, ensuring the valve is turned to the Sealing position. Press Pressure Cook and set the time to 1 minute.

When cooking is complete, turn the valve to the Venting position to release the pressure. Remove the lid and give the mixture a stir.

Serve the compote in dessert bowls and top them with the walnut pieces, or simply spoon the compote over ice cream.

3 medium Granny Smith apples, peeled, cored, and cut into 2–3-inch (5–8 cm) chunks

3 Gala apples (or other red apples) peeled, cored, and cut into 2–3-inch (5–8 cm) chunks

3 large Anjou or Bartlett pears, peeled, cored, and cut into 2–3-inch (5–8 cm) chunks

1 cup (160 g) frozen blueberries

¼ cup (50 g) sugar

1 tablespoon lemon juice

1 teaspoon cinnamon

walnut pieces for topping

BAILEYS LAVA CAKES

YIELD: 4 Servings
HANDS-ON TIME: 10 Minutes
COOKING TIME: 8 Minutes
TOTAL TIME: 20 Minutes
BUTTONS TO USE: Pressure Cook
RELEASE TYPE: Quick Release

If there's only one recipe you make from this book, this should be it! Rich, gooey, warm, and chocolatey with a hint of Baileys® Original Irish Cream . . . these little cakes are irresistible. Just go make them! You will need four 5-ounce (150 ml) ramekins for this recipe.

FOR THE RAMEKINS

2 teaspoons butter, softened

4 teaspoons sugar

FOR THE BATTER

6 tablespoons (85 g) butter

1 cup (200 g) high-quality semi-sweet chocolate chips

½ cup (120 ml) Baileys Original Irish Cream

3 large eggs

1 egg yolk

1 cup (120 g) powdered sugar plus extra for the topping

6 tablespoons (48 g) flour

pinch of salt

raspberries and fresh mint, for serving

TO PREPARE THE RAMEKINS

Smear the inside of the ramekins with the softened butter.

Pour 1 teaspoon of sugar into each ramekin and roll it around to evenly coat the inside of the ramekin with sugar.

TO PREPARE THE LAVA CAKES

In a medium-size microwave-safe dish, combine the butter, chocolate chips, and the Baileys Original Irish Cream. Place the dish in a microwave and heat the mixture on medium power for 3 minutes. Remove the dish and give the mixture a good stir.

In a medium-size bowl, beat the eggs and egg yolk together with a fork. Add the chocolate mixture to the bowl and mix well.

Add the powdered sugar, flour, and salt to the bowl, and mix them well, until a thick batter forms.

continued

Set the Instant Pot steam rack in the Instant Pot inner pot and add 1 cup (240 ml) of water.

Fill each ramekin, almost to the top, with the batter. Place the ramekins on the steam rack. Secure the lid, ensuring the valve is turned to the Sealing position. Press the Pressure Cook button and set the time to 8 minutes.

When cooking is complete, turn the valve to the Venting position to release the pressure. Remove the lid and take out the ramekins, using oven mitts and tongs.

Let the ramekins sit for 5 minutes, and then run a small knife around the inside of each ramekin to loosen the lava cake. Carefully place a small plate over one of the ramekins and invert the plate so that the lava cake comes out of the ramekin and sits upside down on the plate. Repeat this process for the remaining ramekins. Top the lava cakes with sifted powdered sugar and serve them while they're warm with raspberries and fresh mint.

TIP: Remove the cakes from the ramekins as soon as the 5-minute resting time is done to ensure a gooey, liquid center. Allowing the cakes to sit in the ramekins any longer than 5 minutes will result in continued cooking and a more solid center.

CHRISTMAS FUDGE

YIELD: 36 Pieces
HANDS-ON TIME: 15 Minutes
COOKING TIME: 10 Minutes
TOTAL TIME: 25 Minutes
BUTTONS TO USE: Sauté
RELEASE TYPE: None

This white chocolate fudge is loaded with peppermint pieces. It's exactly the kind of fun, light-spirited dessert that can cheer up any dessert table.

3 cups (600 g) white chocolate chips

1 (14-ounce) (397 g) can sweetened condensed milk

2 tablespoons butter

¼ teaspoon salt

1 cup (180 g) finely crushed candy cane or peppermint candy pieces

1 teaspoon vanilla extract

Place the white chocolate chips, sweetened condensed milk, butter, and salt in the Instant Pot inner pot. Press the Sauté button and allow the pot to heat up. Stir the mixture, occasionally, as the pot heats.

When the display reads "Hot," whisk the white chocolate mixture for about 5 minutes, until it has completely melted and blended with the other ingredients.

When the chocolate mixture is completely blended, press the Cancel button to turn off the sauté function. Add the crushed candy cane or peppermint candy pieces and the vanilla to the pot and stir the mixture until it is well combined.

Line an 8 × 8-inch (20 × 20 cm) square baking dish with parchment paper. Make sure the parchment paper overhangs the dish by a couple of inches to allow the fudge to be easily removed. Pour the mixture into the baking dish. Place the dish in the refrigerator to cool for 4 hours.

Lift the fudge out of the pan using the parchment paper overhang. Place the fudge on a cutting board and cut it into 36 pieces. Store the fudge in an airtight container in the refrigerator or freezer.

PUMPKIN CREAM LAVA CAKE

YIELD: 4 Servings

HANDS-ON TIME: 10 Minutes

COOKING TIME: 8 Minutes

TOTAL TIME: 20 Minutes

BUTTONS TO USE: Pressure Cook

RELEASE TYPE: Quick Release

Here's a seasonal take on the ever-popular lava cake. The addition of pumpkin puree, cream, and a touch of allspice really bring out the holiday flavors in this warm, decadent dessert.

TO PREPARE THE RAMEKINS

Smear the inside of the ramekins with the softened butter.

Pour 1 teaspoon of sugar into each ramekin and roll it around to evenly coat the inside of the ramekin with sugar.

TO PREPARE THE LAVA CAKES

In a medium-size microwave-safe dish, combine the butter, white chocolate chips, and cream. Place the dish in the microwave and heat the mixture on medium power for 3 minutes. Remove the dish and give the mixture a good stir.

In a medium-size bowl, beat the eggs and egg yolk together with a fork. Add the white chocolate mixture to the bowl and mix it in well. Add the pumpkin puree to the bowl and mix it into the chocolate until it is fully incorporated.

Add the powdered sugar, flour, nutmeg, and salt to chocolate mixture in the bowl. Mix the ingredients together well until a thick batter forms.

Place the Instant Pot steam rack in the Instant Pot inner pot and add 1 cup (240 ml) of water.

FOR THE RAMEKINS

2 teaspoons butter, softened

4 teaspoons sugar

FOR THE BATTER

8 tablespoons (115 g) butter

1 cup (200 g) high-quality white chocolate chips

½ cup (120 ml) heavy whipping cream

3 medium eggs

1 egg yolk

1 cup (240 g) canned pumpkin puree

1 cup (120 g) powdered sugar

6 tablespoons (50 g) flour

¼ teaspoon freshly grated nutmeg plus more for the topping

pinch of salt

Fill each ramekin almost to the top with the batter. Place the ramekins on the steam rack. Secure the lid, ensuring the valve is turned to the Sealing position. Press the Pressure Cook button and set the timer for 8 minutes.

When cooking is complete, turn the valve to the Venting position to release the pressure. Remove the lid and take out the ramekins, using oven mitts and tongs.

Let the ramekins sit for 5 minutes, and then run a small knife along the inside of each ramekin to loosen the lava cake. Carefully place a small plate over one of the ramekins and invert the plate so that the lava cake comes out of the ramekin and sits upside down on the plate. Repeat this process for the remaining ramekins. Top the lava cakes with a dusting of freshly grated nutmeg and serve them while they're warm.

TIP: Remove the cakes from the ramekins as soon as the 5-minute resting time is done to ensure a gooey, liquid center. Allowing the cakes to sit in the ramekins any longer than 5 minutes will result in continued cooking and a more solid center.

Warm Winter
DRINKS

Hot Buttered Rum 117

Warm Spiced
Mulled Wine 118

Spiked Hot Chocolate 119

Lemon & Rum
Hot Toddy 120

Cranberry Spiced
Black Tea 121

Peppermint
Vanilla Latte 123

Spiced & Spiked
Hot Cider 124

Dulce de Leche Cider
with a Kick 125

Warm Tropical Punch
with a Punch 126

Kahlúa™
Vanilla Latte 127

HOT BUTTERED RUM

YIELD: 4 Drinks
HANDS-ON TIME: 5 Minutes
COOKING TIME: 1 Minute
TOTAL TIME: 7 Minutes
BUTTONS TO USE: Pressure Cook
RELEASE TYPE: Quick Release

One taste and you'll fall in love with this classic, warming winter drink. Spiced rum infused with dark brown sugar, a hint of holiday spices, and just the right amount of butter meld perfectly in a drink so rich it's like having dessert in a mug.

6 tablespoons (50 g) butter

½ cup (100 g) dark brown sugar

2 cinnamon sticks plus 4 cinnamon sticks for garnish

½ teaspoon grated nutmeg

pinch of salt

¾ cup (180 ml) spiced rum

Put all dry ingredients into the Instant Pot inner pot, add 2 cups (480 ml) water, and stir. Secure the lid, ensuring the valve is turned to the Sealing position. Press the Pressure Cook button and set the time to 1 minute.

When cooking is compete, turn the valve to the Venting position to release the pressure. Remove the lid.

Add the rum to the pot and give it a stir or whisk. Ladle the buttered rum into 4 mugs and garnish each with a cinnamon stick.

WARM SPICED MULLED WINE

YIELD: 4 Glasses
HANDS-ON TIME: 5 Minutes
COOKING TIME: 1 Minute
TOTAL TIME: 7 Minutes
BUTTONS TO USE: Pressure Cook
RELEASE TYPE: Quick Release

Holiday flavors and aromas meld beautifully in this festive, soul warming drink—perfect for welcoming your guests or serving with dessert or after dinner.

1 (750 ml) bottle dry red wine

1 medium orange

12 cloves, pressed into the orange

6 juniper berries

6 cardamom pods

2 whole star anise

½ teaspoon nutmeg

½ cup (120 ml) brandy (optional)

sliced oranges and cinnamon sticks for garnish

Add all ingredients, except brandy and cinnamon sticks, to the Instant Pot inner pot and give them a stir.

Secure the lid, ensuring the valve is turned to the Sealing position. Press the Pressure Cook button and set the time to 1 minute.

When cooking is complete, carefully turn the valve to the Venting position to release the pressure. Remove the lid.

Remove the whole spices and clove-studded orange from the pot with a slotted spoon (or strain the mixture through a fine mesh sieve). Serve the mulled wine warm, with a little brandy (optional), slice of orange, and a cinnamon stick for garnish.

TIP: Leave the spiced wine in the Instant Pot on the Warm cycle to keep it at the perfect temperature for your guests.

SPIKED HOT CHOCOLATE

YIELD: 6 Cups (1.5 liters)
HANDS-ON TIME: 5 Minutes
COOKING TIME: 1 Minute
TOTAL TIME: 10 Minutes
BUTTONS TO USE: Pressure Cook
RELEASE TYPE: Natural Release

Holidays are always better with a steaming cup of creamy hot chocolate. The adults at your party will love the extra kick of the spiced rum (optional, of course).

1 (14-ounce) (397 g) can sweetened condensed milk

½ cup unsweetened cocoa powder

1 teaspoon vanilla extract

pinch of salt

1 cup spiced rum (optional)

mini marshmallows for topping (optional)

Place the condensed milk, cocoa powder, vanilla extract, and salt into the Instant Pot inner pot. Add 6 cups (1.5 liters) of water. Whisk together the ingredients until they are well blended. Secure the lid, ensuring the valve is turned to the Sealing position. Press the Pressure Cook button and set the time to 1 minute.

When cooking is complete, let the pot sit for another 5 minutes, and then turn the valve slowly to the Venting position to release the pressure.

Open the lid and stir the mixture until it is well blended. Add the rum, if you like, and stir it in. Ladle the hot chocolate into mugs and top them with mini marshmallows.

LEMON & RUM HOT TODDY

YIELD: 4 Drinks

HANDS-ON TIME: 5 Minutes

COOKING TIME: 1 Minute

TOTAL TIME: 10 Minutes

BUTTONS TO USE: Pressure Cook

RELEASE TYPE: Quick Release

Tea with lemon, honey, and plenty of rum just might be the perfect drink if you're feeling a little under the weather during the holiday season. You can also add a splash of Classic Limoncello (page 151) to your hot toddy, to really kick it up a notch.

4 cups (950 ml) brewed black tea, or tea of your choice

1 tablespoon lemon juice

2 tablespoons honey

1 cup (240 ml) dark rum

lemon slices for garnish

Place the tea, lemon juice, and honey into the Instant Pot inner pot. Stir the mixture well. Secure the lid, ensuring the valve is turned to the Sealing position. Press the Pressure Cook button and set the time to 1 minute.

When cooking is complete, turn the valve to the Venting position to release the pressure.

Remove the lid, add the rum, and stir. Ladle the rum into 4 heatproof glass mugs. Top each mug with a slice of lemon, and serve the toddy piping hot.

CRANBERRY SPICED BLACK TEA

YIELD: 8 Drinks

HANDS-ON TIME: 5 Minutes

COOKING TIME: 1 Minute

TOTAL TIME: 10 Minutes

BUTTONS TO USE: Pressure Cook

RELEASE TYPE: Quick Release

A mug of this healthy, tasty black tea blend will warm you up from the inside out. It will also fill your home with a wonderful wintertime aroma.

1 cup (240 ml) cranberry juice

½ cup (100 g) sugar

2-inch piece fresh ginger, peeled

3 cinnamon sticks

2 whole star anise pods

1 orange, studded with 8 whole cloves

6 black tea bags

orange slices for garnish

Place all the ingredients, except the orange slices, into the Instant Pot inner pot. Add 7 cups (1.5 liters) water. Stir well. Secure the lid, ensuring the valve is turned to the Sealing position. Press the Pressure Cook button and set the time to 1 minute.

When cooking is complete, turn the valve to the Venting position to release the pressure. Remove the lid.

Use a large slotted spoon to lift the orange, tea bags, and whole spices out of the tea and discard them. Ladle the tea into heatproof glass mugs. Top the mugs with a slice of orange and serve the tea while it is hot.

PEPPERMINT VANILLA LATTE

YIELD: 4 Drinks
HANDS-ON TIME: 5 Minutes
COOKING TIME: 1 Minute
TOTAL TIME: 7 Minutes
BUTTONS TO USE: Pressure Cook
RELEASE TYPE: Quick Release

Fill your home with holiday cheer as the aroma of peppermint wafts throughout the air and mugs are filled with this warm, minty latte. It's a good thing it's so easy to make because guests will want seconds for sure!

3 cups (720 ml) very strong brewed coffee

3 cups (720 ml) whole milk

¼ cup (50 g) sugar

1 tablespoon vanilla extract

1½ teaspoons peppermint extract

whipped cream for topping

2 small crushed candy canes for topping

Place the brewed coffee, milk, sugar, vanilla extract, and peppermint extract into the Instant Pot inner pot and stir the mixture well. Secure the lid, ensuring the valve is turned to the Sealing position. Press the Pressure Cook button and set the time to 1 minute.

When cooking is complete, turn the valve to the Venting position to release the pressure. Remove the lid.

Ladle the latte into mugs and top them with a dollop of whipped cream and a sprinkling of the crushed candy canes.

SPICED & SPIKED HOT CIDER

YIELD: 1 Gallon (16 drinks) (about 4 liters)
HANDS-ON TIME: 5 Minutes
COOKING TIME: 1 Minute
TOTAL TIME: 7 Minutes
BUTTONS TO USE: Pressure Cook
RELEASE TYPE: Quick Release

Warm apple cider, infused with winter spices and spiked with some good bourbon, is always a hit at any holiday party. Keep the cider warm in the Instant Pot so your guests can enjoy it all evening, at just the right temperature.

1 gallon (3.75 liters) unfiltered apple cider

3 cinnamon sticks

4 whole star anise

2 tablespoons whole cloves

1 orange, sliced into 1-inch-thick (2.5 cm) slices plus additional slices for garnish

4 cups (950 ml) bourbon

Put the cider, cinnamon sticks, anise, cloves, and orange slices into the Instant Pot inner pot and stir. Secure the lid, ensuring the valve is turned to the Sealing position. Press the Pressure Cook button and set the time to 1 minute.

When cooking is complete, turn the valve to the Venting position to release the pressure. Remove the lid.

Remove the orange and whole spices from the pot using a large slotted spoon (or pour the liquid through a fine sieve into a large bowl, and then pour the liquid back into the Instant Pot to keep it warm.) Add the bourbon and stir. Garnish with additional orange slices. Keep the pot warm in the Instant Pot, so that your guests can serve themselves throughout the evening.

DULCE DE LECHE CIDER WITH A KICK

YIELD: 1 Drink

HANDS-ON TIME: 2 Minutes

COOKING TIME: None

TOTAL TIME: None

BUTTONS TO USE: None

RELEASE TYPE: None

This is a great way to add a sweet and creamy finish to Spiced and Spiked Hot Cider (see the facing page). This recipe is for one drink, but the Spiced and Spiked Hot Cider used for this recipe makes 16 drinks, so feel free to make as many as you wish.

8 ounces (240 ml) warm Spiced & Spiked Hot Cider (page 124)

1 tablespoon Dulce de Leche (page 161)

cinnamon sticks for garnish

Pour 8 ounces (240 ml) of Spiked and Spiced Hot Cider into a heatproof mug.

Add 1 tablespoon of Dulce de Leche and stir. Serve the cider with a cinnamon stick.

WARM TROPICAL PUNCH WITH A PUNCH

YIELD: 6 Drinks

HANDS-ON TIME: 5 Minutes

COOKING TIME: 1 Minute

TOTAL TIME: 7 Minutes

BUTTONS TO USE: Pressure Cook

RELEASE TYPE: Quick Release

If you long to be on a tropical island during the holiday season, this fruit punch, served with a warming hit of vodka, just might make you feel like you've already arrived.

Add all the ingredients, except the vodka and pineapple wedges, to the Instant Pot inner pot and stir. Secure the lid, ensuring the valve is turned to the Sealing position. Press the Pressure Cook button and set the time to 1 minute.

When cooking is complete, turn the valve to the Venting position to release the pressure.

Remove the lid, add the vodka, and stir. Serve the punch in tall, heatproof glass mugs garnished with a pineapple wedge.

2 cups (480 ml) pineapple juice

2 cups (480 ml) orange juice

2 cups (480 ml) cranberry juice

1 tablespoon finely grated fresh ginger

1½ cups (360 ml) vodka

pineapple wedges for garnish

KAHLÚA VANILLA LATTE

YIELD: 6 Drinks
HANDS-ON TIME: 5 Minutes
COOKING TIME: 1 Minute
TOTAL TIME: 7 Minutes
BUTTONS TO USE: Pressure Cook
RELEASE TYPE: Quick Release

The vanilla latte just got a makeover. Add a little Kahlúa liqueur to this classic beverage and let the evening begin!

3 cups (720 ml) strong, brewed coffee

1 cup (240 ml) whole milk

2 cups (480 ml) Kahlúa liqueur

Add the coffee and milk to the Instant Pot inner pot. Stir the mixture and secure the lid, ensuring the valve is turned to the Sealing position. Press the Pressure Cook button and set the time to 1 minute.

When cooking is complete, turn the valve to the Venting position to release the pressure.

Remove the lid and press Cancel to turn off the pot. Press the Sauté button and add the Kahlúa. Stir the mixture for about 1 minute, until it is heated through.

Ladle the drink into heatproof mugs and serve it hot or, alternatively, serve it cold over ice.

Rock Star
LEFTOVERS

Beef & Caramelized
Onion Sandwiches 131

Country Ham Hash 133

Turkey & Wild Rice
Soup 134

Sweet Potato Hummus 135

Sweet Potato
Coconut Soup 137

Quick & Easy
Turkey Pot Pie 138

Turkey & Sweet Potato
Chili 139

Turkey Ramen 140

Cheesy Macaroni
with Ham 142

15-Bean Soup with Ham 144

Turkey Bone Broth 145

Turkey Marsala 147

BEEF & CARAMELIZED ONION SANDWICHES

YIELD: 6 Servings

HANDS-ON TIME: 15 Minutes

COOKING TIME: 10 Minutes

TOTAL TIME: 45 Minutes

BUTTONS TO USE: Sauté and Pressure Cook

RELEASE TYPE: Quick Release

This is a great recipe for leftover Red Wine–Braised Beef Brisket (see page 26) or Beef Pot Roast (page 31). Toast some hoagie rolls and stuff them with warm, tender beef and sweet caramelized onions. A cold beer on the side would make a nice accompaniment.

Press the Sauté button to heat up the Instant Pot inner pot. When the display reads "Hot," add the butter. As soon as butter melts add the sliced onions, Worcestershire sauce, salt, and pepper. Stir well. Sauté the onions for 4 or 5 minutes, or until they just begin to turn soft.

Press Cancel to turn off the sauté function and add ½ cup (120 ml) water to the pot. Secure the lid, ensuring the valve is turned to the Sealing position. Press the Pressure Cook button and set the time to 10 minutes.

When cooking is complete, turn the valve to the Venting position to release the pressure. Remove the lid.

6 tablespoons (85 g) butter

3 pounds (1.3 kg)
yellow onions, sliced into ¼-inch (.5 cm) strips (approximately 5 medium onions)

1 teaspoon Worcestershire sauce

½ teaspoon salt

½ teaspoon pepper

2 pounds (900 g) leftover cooked beef (brisket or pot roast), sliced or shredded

6 hoagie rolls, sliced

continued

Press the Sauté button (you may need to press Cancel first to turn off the warming feature). Sauté the onions until almost all of the liquid has evaporated and the onions just begin to brown, approximately 5 minutes. Add the cooked beef and lightly stir the mixture until it is well combined.

Open the hoagie rolls and place them on a baking sheet. Lightly toast the rolls under the broiler for 3–4 minutes. Pay close attention to the rolls when they're under the broiler so they don't burn.

Remove the hoagie rolls from under the broiler. Place the rolls on individual plates and fill them with the onion and beef mixture. Serve immediately.

COUNTRY HAM HASH

YIELD: 6 Servings

HANDS-ON TIME: 10 Minutes

COOKING TIME: 3 Minutes

TOTAL TIME: 15 Minutes

BUTTONS TO USE: Pressure Cook

RELEASE TYPE: Quick Release

Top this hash with a couple of fried eggs, and you'll have a spectacular breakfast that will get you through the day.

Press the Sauté button to heat up the Instant Pot inner pot. When the display reads "Hot," add the oil to coat the bottom of the pot. Add the onion, potatoes, seasoned salt, pepper, and thyme. Mix well. Let the mixture sit in the pot undisturbed for 2–3 minutes, to lightly brown the potatoes, and then stir the mixture.

Add the red and green bell peppers to the pot and stir them in well. To deglaze the pot, add ¾ cup (180 ml) of water to the pot, making sure to scrape up any brown bits from the bottom of pot, using a wooden spoon. Add the diced ham and stir it into the mixture until it is well combined.

Press the Cancel button to turn off sauté function. Secure the lid, ensuring the valve is turned to the Sealing position. Press the Pressure Cook button and set the time to 3 minutes.

When cooking is complete, turn the valve to the Venting position to release the pressure. Remove the lid.

Stir and then transfer the ham hash to individual plates, using a slotted spoon. Top the hash with fried or over-easy eggs for a complete breakfast.

2 tablespoons vegetable oil

1 medium onion, diced into ½-inch (1 cm) pieces

3 medium russet potatoes, peeled and diced into 1-inch (3 cm) pieces

1 teaspoon seasoned salt

½ teaspoon pepper

½ teaspoon dried thyme

1 medium red bell pepper, seeded and diced into 1-inch (3 cm) pieces

1 medium green bell pepper, seeded and diced into 1-inch (3 cm) pieces

1 pound (450 g) leftover cooked ham (see Succulent Glazed Ham on page 22), diced into ½-inch (1 cm) pieces

TURKEY & WILD RICE SOUP

YIELD: 6 Servings
HANDS-ON TIME: 10 Minutes
COOKING TIME: 25 Minutes
TOTAL TIME: 45 Minutes
BUTTONS TO USE: Soup/Broth
RELEASE TYPE: Natural Release

Leftover turkey, combined with rice, mushrooms, and veggies make a terrific cold-weather soup—comfort food at its best.

Put all the ingredients, except the cream and the turkey, into the Instant Pot inner pot and stir well. Secure the lid, ensuring the valve is turned to the Sealing position. Press the Soup/Broth button and set the time to 25 minutes.

When cooking is complete, let the pot sit for another 10 minutes, and then turn the valve to the Venting position to release any remaining pressure.

Remove the lid and add the cream and cooked turkey. Give the soup a good stir and serve immediately.

1 cup (180 g) uncooked wild rice blend

6 cups (1.5 liters) chicken broth

8 ounces (225 g) sliced mushrooms

1 medium onion, diced

3 stalks celery, sliced crosswise into ½-inch (1 cm) pieces

2 medium carrots, peeled and sliced crosswise into ½-inch (1 cm) pieces

2 garlic cloves, minced

1 teaspoon dried thyme

1 teaspoon salt

½ teaspoon pepper

½ teaspoon cayenne pepper

¾ cup (180 ml) heavy cream

1 pound (450 g) leftover cooked turkey, shredded

SWEET POTATO HUMMUS

YIELD: 4 Cups (450 ml)

HANDS-ON TIME: 5 Minutes

COOKING TIME: 50 Minutes

TOTAL TIME: 75 Minutes

BUTTONS TO USE: Bean/Chili

RELEASE TYPE: Natural Release

Leftover sweet potatoes add a delightful twist to this classic chickpea dip. Make a batch of it after your big holiday dinner and serve it with crunchy rye crackers.

2 cups (160 g) dried chickpeas (also called garbanzo beans)

3 garlic cloves, peeled and smashed

1 tablespoon vegetable oil

1 teaspoon salt

½ teaspoon pepper

¾ cup (180 ml) olive oil, divided

2 cups (480 g) leftover cooked sweet potatoes

¼ cup (30 g) crushed walnut pieces for topping, optional

Place the chickpeas, garlic, and vegetable oil in the Instant Pot inner pot. Add 6 cups (1.5 liters) of water and stir. Secure the lid, ensuring the valve is turned to the Sealing position. Press the Bean/Chili button and set the time to 50 minutes.

When cooking is complete, let the pot sit for another 10 minutes, and then turn the valve to the Venting position to release any remaining pressure. Remove the lid.

Drain the chickpeas in a colander over a large bowl to capture the cooking liquid for later use.

Combine the drained chickpeas, salt, pepper, 4 tablespoons of the olive oil, the sweet potatoes, and ½ cup (120 ml) of the reserved cooking liquid in a food processor. Pulse the food processor to blend the ingredients, and then turn the processor to high. Slowly add the remaining olive oil and additional reserved cooking liquid, as needed, to reach the desired consistency.

Serve the hummus topped with a drizzle of olive oil and topped with crushed walnuts.

SWEET POTATO COCONUT SOUP

YIELD: 6 Servings

HANDS-ON TIME: 5 Minutes

COOKING TIME: 3 Minutes

TOTAL TIME: 15 Minutes

BUTTONS TO USE: Sauté and Pressure Cook

RELEASE TYPE: Slow Release

A healthy blend of leftover sweet potatoes and creamy coconut milk produces a filling and satisfying, thick soup that's perfect for cool fall or winter days. An immersion or stand blender makes it easy to puree the soup to silky perfection.

1 tablespoon olive oil

1 medium onion, diced

2 garlic cloves, minced

2 13½-ounce (400 ml) cans coconut milk

4 cups vegetable broth

1½ teaspoons salt

½ teaspoon pepper

6 cups (1.5 kg) leftover, cooked sweet potatoes, at room temperature

½ cup (120 ml) cream

chopped Italian parsley, for garnish

Press the Sauté button to heat up the Instant Pot inner pot. When the display reads "Hot," add the oil to coat the bottom of the pot. Add the onion and garlic and sauté for 3–4 minutes, until the onion just turns soft.

Add the coconut milk, vegetable broth, salt, and pepper. Stir well, making sure to scrape up any brown bits from the bottom of the pot. Press the Cancel button to turn off the sauté function. Secure the lid, ensuring the valve is turned to the Sealing position. Press the Pressure Cook button and set the time to 3 minutes.

When cooking is complete, let the pot sit for another 5 minutes, and then turn the valve slowly to the Venting position to release any remaining pressure. (See the tip "Slow Release" on page xiii.)

Remove the lid and add the sweet potatoes and cream. Blend the mixture with an immersion blender or in batches in a stand blender until the consistency is very smooth. Serve the soup hot or cold and garnish it with chopped Italian parsley.

QUICK & EASY
TURKEY POT PIE

YIELD: 6 Servings

HANDS-ON TIME: 10 Minutes

COOKING TIME: 8 Minutes

TOTAL TIME: 30 Minutes

BUTTONS TO USE: Pressure Cook

RELEASE TYPE: Natural Release

This rich, savory pot pie is a leftover makeover for extra turkey after your holiday feast. If you use a premade crust, the pie can come together in less than 30 minutes.

Press the Sauté button to heat up the Instant Pot inner pot. When the display reads "Hot," add the oil to coat the bottom of the inner pot. Add the carrots, celery, and onion and sauté the mixture for 3–4 minutes.

Sprinkle the vegetable mixture with the flour, thyme, salt, and pepper, and cook the mixture for 1 minute, stirring it constantly until the vegetables are well coated with flour. Add the chicken broth and stir it well to deglaze the bottom of the pot. Make sure to scrape up any brown bits off the bottom of the pot. Add the pie crust strips one at a time to the pot and stir them gently to distribute the strips throughout the mixture.

Press the Cancel button to turn off the sauté function. Secure the lid, ensuring the valve is turned to the Sealing position. Press Pressure Cook and set the time to 8 minutes.

When cooking is complete, let the pot sit for another 10 minutes, and then slowly turn the valve to the Venting position to release any remaining pressure. (See the tip "Slow Release" on page xiii.) Remove the lid and gently stir in the turkey, cream, and peas. Serve hot.

1 tablespoon olive oil

3 medium carrots, peeled and sliced into ½-inch (1 cm) rounds

4 celery stalks, sliced crosswise into ½-inch (1 cm) pieces

1 medium onion, diced

½ cup (60 g) flour

1 ½ teaspoons dried thyme

½ teaspoon salt

¼ teaspoon pepper

4 cups (950 ml) chicken broth

1 premade (or homemade) pie crust, rolled ½-inch (1 cm) thick and cut into 1 × 3-inch (3 × 8 cm) strips

1 pound (450 g) cooked leftover turkey, shredded

½ cup (120 ml) heavy cream

1 cup (240 g) frozen peas, thawed

TURKEY & SWEET POTATO CHILI

YIELD: 6 Servings

HANDS-ON TIME: 10 Minutes

COOKING TIME: 5 Minutes

TOTAL TIME: 20 Minutes

BUTTONS TO USE: Sauté and Pressure Cook

RELEASE TYPE: Quick Release

This hearty chili is a great way to enjoy Thanksgiving, round #2—and it has a nice spicy kick. If you like, top the chili with a few dried cranberries to give it a festive burst of color.

Press the Sauté button to heat up the Instant Pot inner pot. When the display reads "Hot," add the olive oil to coat the bottom of the pot. Add the onion and garlic and sauté for 2–3 minutes, until the onion is just beginning to soften. Press Cancel to turn off the sauté function.

Add the chili powder, cumin, salt, black beans, sweet potatoes, and chicken broth. Stir the mixture well, making sure to scrape any brown bits off the bottom of the pot.

Secure the lid, ensuring the valve is turned to the Sealing position. Press the Pressure Cook button and set the time to 5 minutes.

When cooking is complete, turn the valve to the Venting position to release the pressure. Remove the lid, stir the chili, and serve it in bowls topped with dried cranberries and green onions.

1 tablespoon olive oil

1 medium onion, diced

2 garlic cloves, minced

3 tablespoons chili powder (or more, if you'd like additional heat)

2 teaspoons cumin

1 teaspoon salt

1 (15-ounce) (425 g) can black beans, drained and rinsed

3 large sweet potatoes, peeled and cut into 2–3-inch (5–8 cm) pieces

6 cups (1.5 liters) chicken broth

dried cranberries for garnish

sliced green onions for garnish

TURKEY RAMEN

YIELD: 6 Servings

HANDS-ON TIME: 5 Minutes

COOKING TIME: 2 Minutes

TOTAL TIME: 15 Minutes

BUTTONS TO USE: Sauté and Pressure Cook

RELEASE TYPE: Quick Release

With a bit of leftover turkey, you can have a delicious, noodley, brothy bowl of gourmet ramen in just a few minutes. And don't forget the fresh toppings. It's all about the toppings!

Press the Sauté button to heat up the Instant Pot inner pot. When the display reads "Hot," add the sesame oil to coat the bottom of the pot. Add the leek, garlic, ginger, and red pepper flakes. Sauté the mixture for 3 minutes, until the leeks start to get soft. Press the Cancel button to turn off the sauté function.

Add the chicken broth, 2 cups (480 ml) of water, soy sauce, and Worcestershire sauce to the pot. Stir well. Secure the lid, ensuring the valve is turned to the Sealing position. Press the Pressure Cook button and set the time to 3 minutes.

When cooking is complete, slowly turn the valve to the Venting position to release the pressure. Remove the lid.

Press the Sauté button (you may have to press Cancel to turn off the warming function first). When soup starts to simmer, add the soba noodles. Stir the mixture to prevent the noodles from sticking together. Simmer the noodles according to the directions on the package (usually 3–6 minutes).

2 teaspoons sesame oil

1 large leek, well rinsed and cut lengthwise in half and crosswise into ½-inch (1 cm) pieces

2 garlic cloves, minced

2 inches (5 cm) fresh ginger, peeled and minced

½ teaspoon red pepper flakes

6 cups (1.5 liters) chicken broth

½ cup (120 ml) soy sauce

2 teaspoons Worcestershire sauce

6 ounces (170 g) uncooked soba noodles (or packaged ramen noodles)

1 pound (450 g) (approximately 6 cups) leftover cooked turkey, cut into bite-size pieces or shredded

sliced fresh jalapeño, for topping

sliced green onions, for topping

chopped cilantro, for topping

hard boiled eggs, sliced in half, for topping

sesame seeds, for topping

Lift the noodles out of the pot with tongs or a spaghetti lifter, and divide them equally among 6 bowls. Place about 1 cup (75 g) of turkey into each bowl of noodles. Stir the broth and ladle it on top of the turkey and noodles. (The broth will be very hot and will warm up the cooked turkey.)

Add the toppings of your choice to the bowls. Serve the ramen while it's hot.

NOTE: Soba noodles are Japanese noodles made from buckwheat flour. They have a subtle earthy or nutty flavor and can be found in specialty grocery stores or online.

CHEESY MACARONI
WITH HAM

YIELD: 6 Servings

HANDS-ON TIME: 5 Minutes

COOKING TIME: 5 Minutes

TOTAL TIME: 15 Minutes

BUTTONS TO USE: Sauté and Pressure Cook

RELEASE TYPE: Slow Release

This is the ultimate comfort food: creamy macaroni loaded with leftover diced ham. Serve the macaroni with a side of Green Beans with Toasted Almonds (see page 75) for a complete meal.

Press the Sauté button to heat up the Instant Pot inner pot. When the display reads "Hot," add the butter. When the butter melts, add the flour and stir the mixture to form a thick paste or roux. Stir continuously until the roux turns golden, and then slowly whisk in 1 cup (240 ml) of water to thin the paste. With a wooden spatula, scrape the bottom of the pot clean. Press the Cancel button to turn off the sauté function.

Add the milk, broth, cream, soup, dry mustard, pepper, and salt. Stir the mixture until it is well blended. Add the macaroni to the pot and stir well. Secure the lid, ensuring the valve is turned to the Sealing position. Press the Pressure Cook button and set the time to 5 minutes.

When cooking is complete, slowly turn the valve to the Venting position to release the pressure (see the tip "Slow Release" on page xiii).

6 tablespoons (85 g) butter

½ cup (60 g) flour

2 cups (480 ml) whole milk

2 cups (480 ml) chicken broth

1 cup (240 ml) heavy cream

1 (10½-ounce) (300 g) can condensed Cream of Cheddar soup

1 teaspoon dry mustard

½ teaspoon pepper

½ teaspoon salt

1 (16-ounce) (450 g) package small elbow macaroni noodles, uncooked

4 cups (450 g) shredded sharp cheddar cheese

1 pound (450 g) cooked ham, diced into ½-inch (1 cm) pieces

1 cup (110 g) Parmesan cheese, shredded, for serving

Remove the lid and stir the macaroni. Add the shredded cheddar cheese, one cup at a time, stirring continuously until all the cheese has been added and is fully incorporated. Stir the ham into the mixture until it is well combined.

Serve the macaroni with a generous sprinkle of Parmesan cheese.

TIP: It is very important to deglaze the pot when making thick and creamy dishes. Do not rush the process of thinning the roux. If it is too thick it will interfere with the proper sealing of the pot. A wooden spatula works best for scraping the bottom clean.

15-BEAN SOUP
WITH HAM

YIELD: 6 Servings

HANDS-ON TIME: 5 Minutes

COOKING TIME: 50 Minutes

TOTAL TIME: 75 Minutes

BUTTONS TO USE: Bean/Chili

RELEASE TYPE: Natural Release

If you're looking for a low-maintenance meal, this recipe is for you. All you need is a 15-bean soup package, including seasonings, and some leftover ham. The bean package is available at most grocery stores and no soaking is required! The result is a delicious, hearty soup that can be pulled together with very little effort.

1 package (20 ounces) (570 g) 15-bean soup blend with flavor packet

6 cups (1.3 liters) chicken broth

1 tablespoon vegetable oil.

1 pound (450 g) leftover cooked ham, diced

Add all the ingredients, except the ham, to the Instant Pot inner pot and stir well. Secure the lid, ensuring the valve is turned to the Sealing position. Press the Bean/Chili button and set the time to 50 minutes.

When cooking is complete, let the pot sit for another 15 minutes, and then turn the valve to the Venting position to release any remaining pressure. Remove the lid, add the ham, and stir. Serve the soup hot.

TURKEY BONE BROTH

YIELD: **8 Cups**
HANDS-ON TIME: **10 Minutes**
COOKING TIME: **120 Minutes**
TOTAL TIME: **175 Minutes**
BUTTONS TO USE: **Soup/Broth**
RELEASE TYPE: **Natural Release**

You can never have enough stock on hand for holiday cooking, and there's no better way to make it than using turkey bones to produce a deeply flavored broth.

Place all the ingredients in the Instant Pot inner pot, along with 8 cups (2 liters) of water, and stir them together. Press the Soup/Broth button and set the time to 120 minutes.

When cooking is complete, let the pot sit until all the pressure is naturally released and the float valve drops. This should take approximately 30 minutes.

Remove the lid and lift out the inner pot, using oven mitts. Pour the broth through a cheesecloth or fine sieve into a large bowl. Cool the broth and store it in individual jars for later use.

2 pounds (900 g) turkey carcass, bones cut into large pieces

1 medium onion, quartered

3 large carrots, cut into large chunks

3 celery stalks, cut into large chunks

4 garlic cloves, smashed but not peeled

1 bunch fresh parsley, rinsed

1 bay leaf

4 sprigs rosemary

1 teaspoon salt

TURKEY MARSALA

YIELD: 4 Servings

HANDS-ON TIME: 5 Minutes

COOKING TIME: 5 Minutes

TOTAL TIME: 15 Minutes

BUTTONS TO USE: Sauté and Pressure Cook

RELEASE TYPE: Quick Release

Here's a lightning-quick, completely satisfying way to transform leftover turkey into a meal that has all the richness and flavor of classic Chicken Marsala.

- 2 tablespoons butter
- 2 tablespoons olive oil
- 1 pound (450 g) sliced cremini mushrooms
- 3 medium shallots, thinly sliced
- 3 garlic cloves, minced
- ½ cup (120 ml) chicken broth
- ½ cup (120 ml) Marsala wine (or other dry red wine)
- 2 tablespoons cornstarch mixed with 2 tablespoons water, for the slurry
- leftover turkey breast, sliced into ½-inch-thick (1 cm) slices
- 1 (12-ounce) (340g) bag egg noodles, prepared according to package instructions

Press the Sauté button to heat up the Instant Pot inner pot. When the display reads "Hot," add the butter and olive oil. When the butter melts, add the mushrooms, shallots, and garlic. Sauté the mixture for about 5 minutes, until the mushrooms begin to release their juices. Press the Cancel button to turn off the sauté function.

To deglaze the bottom of the pot, add the broth and wine. Stir well, making sure to scrape up any brown bits from the bottom of the pot. Secure the lid, ensuring the valve is turned to the Sealing position. Press the Pressure Cook button and set the time to 5 minutes.

When cooking is complete, turn the valve to the Venting position to release the pressure. Remove the lid.

Select the sauté function (you may have to press Cancel to turn off the warming function.) Add the slurry and stir the mixture constantly until the desired thickness is reached. Add the turkey slices, submerging them in the mixture and heating it for another 2 minutes until the turkey is heated through. Serve the Turkey Marsala over warm egg noodles.

Gifts from the
KITCHEN

Classic Limoncello 151

Sea Salt Popcorn 152

Homemade
Strawberry Jam 153

It's Actually Really
Good Fruitcake 154

Chocolate Peanut Butter
Buckeyes 156

Apple Pie Moonshine 159

Lemon Curd 160

Dulce de Leche 161

Peppermint Bark 162

Homemade
Apple Butter 164

Spiced Cashews 165

Homemade
Vanilla Extract 166

Marshmallow Fudge 167

CLASSIC LIMONCELLO

YIELD: Approximately 750 ml

HANDS-ON TIME: 5 Minutes

COOKING TIME: 30 Minutes

TOTAL TIME: 60 Minutes

BUTTONS TO USE: Pressure Cook

RELEASE TYPE: Quick Release

Your friends and family will love drizzling this tart, lemony liqueur over ice cream, mixing it into marinades, and maybe spiking their tea. You will need two 16-ounce (475 ml) canning jars to make this recipe. (See "Pot-in-Pot Cooking Method" on page xiv.)

peels of 4 lemons, all white pith removed

1 (750 ml) bottle of vodka

1 cup (240 ml) simple syrup (1 cup [200 g] sugar dissolved in 1 cup [240 ml] water)

Put half of the lemon peels into each of the canning jars. Pour the vodka over the peels, filling the jars until just below the jar threads. Secure the canning jar lids until just barely tight.

Position the Instant Pot steam rack in the Instant Pot inner pot and add 1 cup (240 ml) water. Place the 2 canning jars on top of the steam rack.

Secure lid, ensuring the valve is turned to the Sealing position. Press Pressure Cook and set the time to 30 minutes.

When cooking is complete, turn the valve to the Venting position. Remove the lid when all pressure has released.

Carefully remove the canning jars from the pot, using tongs and hot pads. The jars will be very hot and bubbling at this point. Place them on a heatproof surface and let them cool completely to room temperature. Once the jars are cool, remove the lids and add the desired amount of simple syrup: 2 tablespoons per jar for very tart Limoncello and ½ cup (120 ml) per jar for sweeter Limoncello. Mix well.

Transfer the Limoncello to decorative bottles for gift giving.

SEA SALT POPCORN

YIELD:	Approximately 8 Cups (2 liters) Popped Corn
HANDS-ON TIME:	2 Minutes
COOKING TIME:	Approximately 5 Minutes
TOTAL TIME:	10 Minutes
BUTTONS TO USE:	Sauté (high)
RELEASE TYPE:	None

If you're heading to a party and need a gift to bring, here's one that can be pulled together quickly. Make a batch of sea salt popcorn, bag it up, and tie it with a festive bow. You're all set!

3 tablespoons high smoke point oil, such as grape seed or corn oil (*do not use butter!*)

½ cup (275 g) popcorn kernels

2 teaspoons sea salt

Press the Sauté button, repeatedly, until it is on High Sauté, to heat up the Instant Pot inner pot. When the display reads "Hot," add the oil to coat the bottom. Add the corn kernels to the pot and stir until they're well coated.

Cover the pot with a non-sealing lid, such as a glass lid or a large metal lid.

The corn should start popping within 2–3 minutes. Listen carefully and when the popping noise reduces to 1 pop every 5 seconds, turn the pot off. Shake the pot a little to ensure that all kernels have popped.

Lift the lid and pour the popcorn into a large bowl. Remove any unpopped kernels and sprinkle the popcorn with sea salt. Let the popcorn cool, then bag and tie it with a bow.

HOMEMADE STRAWBERRY JAM

YIELD: 3 Cups (720 ml)

HANDS-ON TIME: 5 Minutes

COOKING TIME: 2 Minutes

TOTAL TIME: 45 Minutes

BUTTONS TO USE: Pressure Cook

RELEASE TYPE: Natural Release

Your friends don't need to know how easy it is to make this strawberry jam. Just hand them a jar and graciously accept their praises.

2 pounds (900 g) fresh strawberries, hulled and cut in half

½ cup (100 g) sugar

4 tablespoons lemon juice

2 tablespoons cornstarch mixed with 2 tablespoons water, if necessary, for the slurry

Place the strawberries in the Instant Pot inner pot and sprinkle them with the sugar. Let the pot sit for 15 minutes (the sugar will draw liquid out of the strawberries, which is necessary for the pot to pressurize properly).

Add the lemon juice and stir the mixture. Secure the lid, ensuring the valve is turned to the Sealing position. Press the Pressure Cook button and set the time to 2 minutes.

When cooking is complete, let the pot sit for another 15 minutes, and then turn the valve to the Venting position to release the pressure. Remove the lid and give the mixture a good stir.

Depending on the amount of liquid released from the strawberries, you may need to add a slurry to the mix in order to thicken the jam. Simply press the Sauté button and bring the strawberry mixture to a simmer. Add the slurry to the mixture, stirring it constantly, until the desired thickness is reached, and then press Cancel to turn off the sauté function. Let the jam cool before spooning it into decorative jars for gift giving.

IT'S ACTUALLY REALLY GOOD FRUITCAKE

YIELD: Approximately 8 Slices

HANDS-ON TIME: 10 Minutes

COOKING TIME: 61 Minutes

TOTAL TIME: 90 Minutes

BUTTONS TO USE: Pressure Cook

RELEASE TYPE: Quick

Giving a fruitcake as a gift used to be a joke (most of them were inedible), and yet it is traditional to make and exchange these cakes over the holidays. Well, the joke's over now; this recipe delivers a moist, dense loaf, loaded with dried fruit. It is delicious from start to finish, so save this gift for your favorite people. They deserve it. You will need a 7-inch (18 cm) springform pan to make the cake. (See "Pot-in-Pot Cooking Method" on page xiv.)

TO HYDRATE THE FRUIT

Add all the fruit and the apple juice to the Instant Pot inner pot. Stir the mixture well. Secure the lid, ensuring the valve is turned to the Sealing position. Press the Pressure Cook button and set the time to 1 minute.

When cooking is complete, turn the valve to the Venting position to release the pressure. Remove the lid and pour the fruit mixture into a large bowl.

TO HYDRATE THE FRUIT

½ cup (80 g) dried, sweetened pineapple, chopped into ½-inch (1 cm) pieces

½ cup (85 g) pitted dates, chopped into ½-inch (1 cm) pieces

½ cup (100 g) dried apricots, chopped into ½-inch (1 cm) pieces

½ cup (80 g) dried cherries, chopped into ½-inch (1 cm) pieces

½ cup (75 g) golden raisins

1 tablespoon crystallized ginger

¾ cup (180 ml) apple juice

TO MAKE THE CAKE

In a medium-size bowl, combine the butter, brown sugar, salt, cinnamon, nutmeg, baking powder, eggs, flour, cocoa powder, corn syrup, and apple juice. Mix well. It will be very thick.

Add the mixture to the fruit mixture and mix well. It will be thick. Fold in the nuts and stir until they are mixed in.

Spray the springform pan with cooking spray. Scoop the batter into the springform pan. It should fill the pan almost to the top.

Position the Instant Pot steam rack in the Instant Pot inner pot and add 1 cup (240 ml) water. Place the springform pan onto the steam rack. Secure the lid, ensuring the valve is turned to the Sealing position. Press the Pressure Cook button and set the time to 60 minutes.

When cooking is complete, turn the valve to the Venting position to release the pressure. Remove the lid when all the pressure is released and carefully remove the springform pan, using kitchen mitts. Put the springform pan on a cooling rack and let it cool completely. Remove the rim of the springform pan and use a spatula to remove the cake from the bottom of pan. It should release easily. When the cake has completely cooled, wrap it in decorative plastic wrap and give to your most special friends!

FOR THE CAKE

½ cup (115 g) butter, melted

1 cup (200 g) brown sugar

½ teaspoon salt

½ teaspoon ground cinnamon

¼ teaspoon grated nutmeg

1 teaspoon baking powder

2 large eggs, beaten

1 cup (120 g) flour

2 tablespoons cocoa powder

3 tablespoons dark corn syrup

¼ cup (60 ml) apple juice

1 cup (120 g) chopped nuts of choice

cooking spray

CHOCOLATE PEANUT BUTTER BUCKEYES

YIELD: Approximately 40 Balls

HANDS-ON TIME: 15 Minutes

COOKING TIME: 5 Minutes

TOTAL TIME: 30 Minutes

BUTTONS TO USE: Sauté

RELEASE TYPE: None

Perfectly melted chocolate, using the Instant Pot as a double boiler, makes it easy to make this traditional holiday treat. For a memorable gift, pack these luscious Buckeyes in a beautiful tin.

1½ cups (385 g) creamy peanut butter

½ cup (115 g) softened butter

1 pound (450 g) powdered sugar

1 teaspoon vanilla

2 cups (400 g) semi-sweet chocolate chips

⅛ teaspoon cayenne pepper

In a large bowl, mix together the peanut butter, butter, powdered sugar, and vanilla until the mixture is well blended. Shape the mixture into 1-inch (3 cm) balls. Set them aside.

Pour 2 cups of water into the Instant Pot inner pot and press the Sauté button to heat up the water. Place 1½ cups (50 g) of the semi-sweet chocolate chips in a heatproof bowl that is slightly wider than the opening of the Instant Pot. The bowl should sit on top of the Instant Pot opening, not in the pot.

When the water starts to simmer, set the bowl on top of the Instant Pot opening (you will not be using the lid for this recipe). The chocolate will gradually begin to melt. As the chocolate melts, whisk the mixture to combine the melted chocolate.

As soon as the chocolate melts, press the Cancel button to turn off the sauté function. Carefully remove the bowl, making sure to avoid any excess steam that comes out from under the bowl. Place the bowl on a heatproof surface and whisk in the remaining ½ cup (50 g) of the chocolate chips until they melt, then add the cayenne pepper and blend well. If needed, return the bowl to the top of the Instant Pot and press the Sauté button to heat the water in order to melt any remaining unmelted chocolate.

Use a toothpick to pick up each peanut butter ball and dip it halfway into the chocolate. As you lift the ball out of the chocolate, let the excess drain back into the bowl.

Place the chocolate-dipped peanut butter balls on a cookie sheet lined with parchment paper to cool. Store the Buckeyes in an airtight container in the refrigerator and package them for gifts.

TIP: Insert the toothpicks at a slight angle to prevent the peanut butter balls from slipping off during the dipping process. As soon as you place the dipped balls onto the cookie sheet to cool, remove the toothpicks

APPLE PIE MOONSHINE

YIELD: 20 Cups (4.75 liters)

HANDS-ON TIME: 5 Minutes

COOKING TIME: 60 Minutes

TOTAL TIME: 70 Minutes

BUTTONS TO USE: Sauté and Pressure Cook

RELEASE TYPE: Natural Release

You might make a few new friends when everyone hears that you're making apple pie moonshine for holiday gifts. Don't worry—this recipe makes enough moonshine to fill approximately 10 mason jars, so no one will be left out!

1 gallon (3.75 liters) apple cider

1 (12-ounce) (355 ml) can frozen apple juice concentrate

½ cup (100 g) brown sugar

3 cinnamon sticks

1 cup spiced rum

1 (750 ml) bottle vodka or grain alcohol

Place the apple cider, frozen apple juice concentrate, brown sugar, and the cinnamon sticks in the Instant Pot inner pot. Press the Sauté button to heat the pot. Heat the mixture, stirring it frequently, until the sugar has dissolved. Press Cancel to turn off the sauté function.

Secure the lid, ensuring the valve is turned to the Sealing position. Press the Pressure Cook button and set the time to 60 minutes.

When cooking is complete, let the pot naturally release until the float valve (the pin next to the venting knob) drops down into the lid. Remove the lid when the pressure is completely released.

Remove the cinnamon sticks using tongs. Add the rum and vodka (or grain alcohol) and mix well. Let the moonshine cool before transferring it to canning jars for gifts.

NOTE: The hard alcohol gets added *after* the pressure-cooking process.

LEMON CURD

YIELD: Approximately
2 Cups (480 ml)
HANDS-ON TIME: 5 Minutes
COOKING TIME: 3 Minutes
TOTAL TIME: 15 Minutes
BUTTONS TO USE: Pressure Cook
RELEASE TYPE: Natural Release

This delicious gift can be blended into yogurt or used as a dessert topping. Lemon zest is a crucial ingredient—so don't skip it! You'll need an ovenproof glass bowl that fits in your Instant Pot to make the lemon curd. (See "Pot-in-Pot Cooking Method" on page xiv.)

3 large eggs

3 large egg yolks

1 cup (200 g) sugar

½ cup (115 g) softened butter

1 cup (240 ml) fresh lemon juice (using fresh lemon juice is well worth the effort here)

1 teaspoon fresh lemon zest

In an ovenproof glass bowl, whisk together the eggs, egg yolks, and sugar until the mixture is well blended and the eggs have turned a light, pale-yellow color. Add the softened butter and whisk the mixture until the butter is well incorporated.

Add the lemon juice and lemon zest to the bowl and blend it into the mixture. Cover the bowl very tightly with aluminum foil.

Position the Instant Pot steam rack in the Instant Pot inner pot and add 1 cup (240 ml) of water to the pot. Place the covered bowl on top of the steam rack. Secure the lid, ensuring the valve is turned to the Sealing position. Press the Pressure Cook button and set the time to 3 minutes.

When cooking is complete, let the pot sit for 10 minutes, then turn the valve to the Venting to release any remaining pressure. Remove the lid and carefully lift out the bowl, using oven mitts.

Remove the foil from the bowl. Whisk the curd until it is smooth. Spoon the curd into jars. Secure the lids and refrigerate the jars until you are ready to give them away.

TIP: For added charm, include a handwritten recipe card for Lemon Curd Tart (page 99) with the jar of bright and tangy lemon curd.

DULCE
DE LECHE

YIELD: 14 Ounces (400 g)

HANDS-ON TIME: 2 Minutes

COOKING TIME: 30 Minutes

TOTAL TIME: 45 Minutes

BUTTONS TO USE: Pressure Cook

RELEASE TYPE: Quick Release

Your gift will be the hit of the party when you present a jar of this rich caramel dessert topping. You can also add a heaping spoonful of dulce de leche to an after-dinner cup of joe for a rich, decadent drink. You will need a 16-ounce (475 ml) canning jar for this recipe. (See "Pot-in-Pot Cooking Method" on page xiv.)

1 (14-ounce) (397 g) can sweetened condensed milk

Place the Instant Pot steam rack in the Instant Pot inner pot. Pour the can of sweetened condensed milk into the canning jar, lightly screw the lid on, and place it on top of the steam rack. Fill the inner pot with water until the water comes up to 1 inch (3 cm) below the top of the canning jar.

Secure the Instant Pot lid, ensuring the valve is turned to the Sealing position. Press the Pressure Cook button and set the time to 30 minutes.

When cooking is complete, turn the valve to the Venting position to release the pressure. Remove the lid and carefully remove the jar using tongs or oven mitts.

Allow the jar to cool to room temperature.

PEPPERMINT BARK

YIELD: Approximately 2 Pounds (900 g)

HANDS-ON TIME: 5 Minutes

COOKING TIME: 10 Minutes

TOTAL TIME: 20 Minutes plus 2 hours cooling time

BUTTONS TO USE: Sauté

RELEASE TYPE: None

This rich chocolate brittle topped with crushed candy canes might just be the best food gift of the season. Using the Instant Pot for a double boiler makes melting the chocolate a breeze.

cooking spray

1 (12-ounce) (350 g) bag high-quality semi-sweet chocolate chips

1 teaspoon peppermint extract

1 (12-ounce) (350 g) bag high-quality white chocolate chips

4 candy canes, crushed

Line a 9 × 13-inch (23 × 33 cm) rimmed baking sheet with aluminum foil. Spray the foil with cooking spray. Set the baking sheet aside.

Pour 2 cups (480 ml) of water into the Instant Pot inner pot and press the Sauté button to heat up the water. Place 1½ cups (265 g) of the semi-sweet chocolate chips into a heatproof bowl that is slightly wider than the opening to your Instant Pot. The bowl should sit on top of the Instant Pot opening, not in it.

When the water starts to simmer, set the bowl on top of the Instant Pot opening (you will not be using the lid for this recipe). The chocolate will gradually begin to melt. As the chocolate melts, whisk the mixture to combine the melted chocolate.

As soon as the chocolate melts, press the Cancel button to turn off the sauté function. Carefully remove the glass bowl, making sure to avoid any excess steam that comes out from under the bowl. Place the bowl on a heatproof surface and whisk in the remaining ½ cup (85 g) of the chocolate chips until they melt. If needed, return the bowl to the top of the Instant Pot and press the Sauté button to heat the water in order to melt any remaining un-melted chocolate. Add the peppermint extract and blend it in well. Pour the melted chocolate chips onto the prepared baking sheet. Set the sheet aside until the chocolate has mostly set, approximately 10 minutes.

Clean the bowl and add all but ½ cup (85 g) of the white chocolate chips to the bowl. Press the Sauté button to heat up the water in the Instant Pot inner pot. There should still be warm water in the pot, but add an additional cup if needed.

When the water starts to simmer, set the bowl on top of the Instant Pot opening. The white chocolate will gradually begin to melt. As the white chocolate melts, whisk the mixture to combine the melted white chocolate.

As soon as the white chocolate melts, press the Cancel button to turn off the sauté function. Carefully remove the glass bowl, making sure to avoid any excess steam that comes out from under the bowl. Place the bowl on a heatproof surface and whisk in the remaining ½ cup (85 g) of the white chocolate chips until they've melted. If needed, return the bowl to the top of the Instant Pot and press the Sauté button to heat the water to melt any remaining un-melted chocolate. Pour the melted white chocolate chips onto the semi-sweet chocolate layer and immediately top the chocolate with the crushed candy canes.

Let the bark sit at room temperature for 1–2 hours until it has fully set. Remove the bark from the baking sheet and break it into pieces. Package the bark for gifts.

HOMEMADE APPLE BUTTER

YIELD: Approximately 6 Cups (1.5 liters)

HANDS-ON TIME: 10 Minutes

COOKING TIME: 8 Minutes

TOTAL TIME: 20 Minutes

BUTTONS TO USE: Pressure Cook and Sauté

RELEASE TYPE: Quick Release

Apple butter makes a great topping for nearly everything—toast, ice cream, yogurt, fresh fruit . . . you name it. See how many creative ways your friends use this delicious gift!

Place all the ingredients in the Instant Pot inner pot and stir them well. Secure the lid, ensuring the valve is turned to the Sealing position. Press the Pressure Cook button and set the time to 8 minutes.

When cooking is complete, turn the valve to the Venting position to release the pressure. Press the Cancel button to turn off the pot.

Open the lid and stir the mixture. Press the Sauté button and continue to stir the apple mixture until it has thickened just enough to hold a spoon in a mound. For a finer texture, blend the apple butter with an immersion blender. Press the Cancel button and transfer the apple butter to a bowl. Let it cool in the refrigerator, and then spoon the apple butter into individual jars for gift giving.

5 pounds apples of choice (Yellow Delicious, Granny Smith, and Gala are good choices), peeled, cored, and cut into large slices.

1 cup (240 ml) apple cider vinegar

1 cup (200 g) brown sugar

1 tablespoon maple syrup

1 teaspoon vanilla extract

½ teaspoon ground cinnamon

¼ teaspoon ground nutmeg

¼ teaspoon ground allspice

SPICED CASHEWS

YIELD: 4 Cups (950 ml)

HANDS-ON TIME: 5 Minutes

COOKING TIME: 10 Minutes plus 15 minutes in oven

TOTAL TIME: 40 Minutes

BUTTONS TO USE: Sauté and Pressure Cook

RELEASE TYPE: Quick Release

A jar of homemade, spiced cashews is a great alternative to bringing a bottle of wine to a party.

2 tablespoons butter

4 cups (600 g) whole cashews

1 teaspoon seasoned salt

1 teaspoon dried tarragon

½ teaspoon pepper

¼ teaspoon cayenne pepper

cooking spray

Press the Sauté button to heat the Instant Pot inner pot. When the display reads "Hot," add the butter. As soon as the butter melts, add the remaining ingredients. Sauté the mixture, stirring it constantly for 2 minutes, until the cashews are well coated. Press Cancel to turn off the sauté function.

Add ¾ cup (120 ml) water to the pot, scraping up any brown bits from the bottom of the pot with a wooden spoon. Secure the lid, ensuring the valve is turned to the Sealing position. Press the Pressure Cook button and set the time to 10 minutes.

While the cashews are cooking, preheat the oven to 425°F (220°C). Spray a rimmed baking sheet with cooking spray.

When cooking is complete, turn the valve to the Venting position to release the pressure. Remove the lid and transfer the cashews to the baking sheet using a slotted spoon. Spread the cashews in one layer on the baking sheet and place it in the oven for 15 minutes, turning the sheet once.

Remove the tray from the oven and let the cashews cool completely before packaging them.

HOMEMADE VANILLA EXTRACT

YIELD: 2 Cups
HANDS-ON TIME: 5 Minutes
COOKING TIME: 60 Minutes
TOTAL TIME: 120 Minutes
BUTTONS TO USE: Pressure Cook
RELEASE TYPE: Natural Release

Your friends will be amazed when you hand them a beautiful bottle of homemade vanilla, and it couldn't be easier (or more economical) to make. You will need a 16-ounce (475– ml) heat-proof canning jar for this recipe. (See "Pot-in-Pot Cooking Method" on page xiv.)

4 grade B vanilla beans
(these can be found online and are less expensive than grade A vanilla beans sold in grocery stores)
2 cups (480 ml) 80-proof vodka

Slice the vanilla beans lengthwise, and then cut each of them in half. Place the vanilla beans in the canning jar and fill it up to the thread lines with vodka. Place the lid on the jar and tighten it.

Position the Instant Pot steam rack in the Instant Pot inner pot and add 1 cup (240 ml) of water. Place the canning jar onto the steam rack and secure the lid, ensuring the valve is turned to the Sealing position. Press the Pressure Cook button and set the time to 60 minutes.

When cooking is complete, let the pot sit for another 60 minutes, and then turn the valve to the Venting position to release any additional pressure.

Remove the lid of the pot and carefully remove the canning jar, using tongs or oven mitts. The jar will be very hot. Place the jar on a cooling rack or hot pad and allow it to cool completely.

Transfer the vanilla to decorative bottles, and place one or two of the vanilla beans into each bottle. Store the bottles in a cool, dry place.

MARSHMALLOW FUDGE

YIELD: 36 Pieces

HANDS-ON TIME: 15 Minutes

COOKING TIME: 10 Minutes

TOTAL TIME: 25 Minutes

BUTTONS TO USE: Sauté

RELEASE TYPE: None

The marshmallows in this recipe give the fudge a nice lift, and it's sure to be a hit with the lucky person who receives it as a gift.

2 cups (400 g) semisweet chocolate chips

1 cup (200 g) milk chocolate chips

1 (14-ounce) (397 g) can sweetened condensed milk

2 tablespoons butter

¼ teaspoon salt

2 cups (100 g) mini marshmallows

1 cup (120 g) walnut pieces, salted and toasted

1 teaspoon vanilla extract

Put semisweet chocolate chips, milk chocolate chips, sweetened condensed milk, butter, and salt into the Instant Pot inner pot. Press the Sauté button and allow the pot to heat up, stirring the mixture occasionally as the pot heats.

When the display reads "Hot," whisk the chocolate mixture together until it has completely melted and blended, approximately 5 minutes.

When the chocolate mixture is blended, press the Cancel button to turn off the sauté function. Fold in and blend the marshmallows in the chocolate mixture using a silicone spatula.

When the mixture is fully blended, add the walnut pieces and vanilla, and stir until the mixture is well combined.

Pour the fudge into an 8 × 8-inch (20 × 20 cm) square baking pan lined with parchment paper. Make sure the parchment paper overhangs the pan by a couple of inches to allow the fudge to be easily removed. Place the fudge in the refrigerator and let it cool for 4 hours.

Lift the fudge out of the pan using the parchment paper. Place the fudge on a cutting board and cut it into 36 pieces. Store it in an airtight container in the refrigerator or freezer.

ABOUT THE AUTHOR

Heather Schlueter, J.D., is an attorney turned CEO turned food blogger and author. She loves cooking for her immediate and extended family, which often includes anywhere from 8 to 20 people, six nights per week.

Heather believes that mealtime is a time for love, laughter, happiness, and bonding. This belief drives her passion for serving home-cooked, fresh, and comforting family meals. Her love of writing and communication is the foundation on which she has built her successful professional career. Her blog, *The Spicy Apron*, combines her passion for cooking and writing in one place. Heather has crafted her cooking style and built her blog around the motto: Keep it Simple. Keep it Tasty. Keep it Easy to Clean. She is passionate about sharing her years of cooking knowledge with others to help them make mealtime an easy, fun, and enjoyable experience.

Heather lives in Scottsdale, Arizona, with her husband, their eight children (although several are grown and out of the house), and their golden doodle, Bentley. Find more from Heather at www.TheSpicyApron.com and on *The Spicy Apron Cooking Show* YouTube channel. Also check out Heather's other Instant Pot authorized cookbook, *Cooking with Your Instant Pot® Mini*, available at your favorite book seller and online.

ACKNOWLEDGMENTS

This cookbook is a delicious work of art thanks to many dedicated people. First and foremost, thank-you to my wonderful husband who always has my back and was more than willing to clean my Instant Pot hundreds of times so I could get all the recipes in this book *just* right. To my entire family who enthusiastically devoured all of my holiday creations even in the midst of springtime. There's nothing quite like turkey, sweet potatoes, and pumpkin pasta as spring gives way to summer! Thank you to the Instant Pot gang and community who continue to give me unwavering support. And a great big thank-you to Nicole Fisher and the entire team at Sterling Publishing whose attention to detail, flair for beauty, and sheer determination to put out the very best holiday cookbook on the shelves this season produced a book that far exceeded my expectations (and I've got high expectations!)

INDEX

Accu Slim Sous Vide Immersion Circulator, xv
Acorn Squash with Shallots & Grapes, 55
Altitude, cooking times at, xi
Appetizers and starters, 1–19
    Asian Chicken Wings, 14–15
    Bourbon-Glazed Meatballs the Easy Way, 17
    Buffalo Chicken Dip, 8–9
    Caramelized Onion & Cranberry Dip, 7
    Classic Deviled Eggs, 12–13
    Holiday Hummus, 11
    Salted Boiled Peanuts, 3
    Shrimp with Butter & Garlic, 18
    Sweet & Spicy Cocktail Sausages, 19
    Tender Stuffed Mushrooms, 5–6
    Warm & Creamy Spinach Artichoke Dip, 10
    Warm Brie with Honey & Apples, 2
Apples
    Apple-Orange Chutney, 77
    Apple Pie Moonshine, 159
    Chunky Cinnamon Applesauce, 56
    Dulce de Leche Cider with a Kick, 125
    Homemade Apple Butter, 164
    Spiced & Spiked Hot Cider, 124
    Spiced Apple Crisp, 106
    Stuffed Cinnamon Walnut Apples, 103
    Warm Brie with Honey & Apples, 2
    Warm Fruit & Nut Compote, 107
Artichokes, in Warm & Creamy Spinach Artichoke
    Dip, 10
Asian Chicken Wings, 14–15

Bacon, white beans with rosemary and, 58–59
Baileys Lava Cakes, 109–110
Beans and other legumes
    about: Bean/Chili button, xi
    15-Bean Soup with Ham, 144

Green Beans with Toasted Almonds, 75
Holiday Hummus, 11
No-Soak Black Beans with Ginger & Nutmeg, 83
Sweet Potato Hummus, 135
Turkey & Sweet Potato Chili, 139
White Beans with Bacon & Rosemary, 58–59
Beef
    about: crisping, xiii; Meat/Stew button, xiii
    Beef & Caramelized Onion Sandwiches, 131–132
    Beef Pot Roast, 31
    Beef Stroganoff, 37
    Beer-Braised Shredded Beef, 38
    Bourbon-Glazed Meatballs the Easy Way, 17
    Red Wine–Braised Beef Brisket, 26–27
    Sous Vide Filet Mignon, 47–49
    Beer-Braised Shredded Beef, 38
Beet salad, 81–82
Berries. *See also* Cranberries
    Berry Cobbler with Granola Topping, 95
    Homemade Strawberry Jam, 153
    Warm Fruit & Nut Compote, 107
Best Beet Salad, 81–82
Beverages. *See* Drinks
Bone broth, turkey, 145
Bourbon-Glazed Meatballs the Easy Way, 17
Bread
    Leek, Parsnip & Herb Brioche Dressing, 64–65
    Sausage & Sage Stuffing, 71–72
    Upside Down, Nutty, Pull-Apart Cinnamon Rolls,
        87–88
Broth, turkey bone, 145
Brownies, chocolate-mint, 93–94
Brussels sprouts with pomegranate, 66–67
Buckeyes, chocolate peanut butter, 156–157
Buffalo Chicken Dip, 8–9
Buttons on Instant Pot, xi–xii

Cake. *See* Desserts
Cake button, xi
Cancel button, xii
Caramelized Onion & Cranberry Dip, 7
Cashews, spiced, 165
Cauliflower
    Cauliflower Au Gratin, 62
    Winter Vegetable Mix, 68
Cheese
    Cauliflower Au Gratin, 62
    Cheesy Macaroni with Ham, 142–143
    Creamy Cheesecake with a Touch of Orange, 96–97
    Red Velvet Cheesecake, 104–105
    Tender Stuffed Mushrooms, 5–6
    Warm Brie with Honey & Apples, 2
Cherries jubilee, warm, 89
Chocolate
    Baileys Lava Cakes, 109–110
    Chocolate Peanut Butter Buckeyes, 156–157
    Christmas Fudge, 111
    Marshmallow Fudge, 167
    Peppermint Bark, 162–163
    Spiked Hot Chocolate, 119
    Super-Simple Chocolate Mint Brownies, 93–94
    Chunky Cinnamon Applesauce, 56
Cider, dulce de leche with a kick, 125
Cider, spiced and spiked hot, 124
    Cinnamon
    Chunky Cinnamon Applesauce, 56
    Stuffed Cinnamon Walnut Apples, 103
    Upside Down, Nutty, Pull-Apart Cinnamon Rolls,
        87–88
Citrus
    Apple-Orange Chutney, 77
    Classic Limoncello, 151
    Creamy Cheesecake with a Touch of Orange, 96–97
    Lemon and Rum Hot Toddy, 120
    Lemon Curd, 160
    Lemon Curd Tart, 99–100
    Warm Tropical Punch with a Punch, 126
Classic Deviled Eggs, 12–13
Classic Limoncello, 151
Classic Mashed Potatoes, 73
Cleaning Instant Pot, xiv
Cobbler, berry with granola topping, 95
Cocktail sausages, sweet and spicy, 19

Coconut, in Sweet Potato Coconut Soup, 137
Coffee
    Kahlúa Vanilla Latte, 127
    Peppermint Vanilla Latte, 123
Compote, warm fruit and nut, 107
Cooking suggestions, xii–xv. *See also* Pressure
    button functions, xi–xii
    cornstarch uses, xii
    crisping things first, xiii
    filling inner pot, xiv
    ingredient brands affecting results, xiv
    pot-in-pot cooking, xiv–xv
    sauté function, xii, xv
    sous vide cooking, xv
    thickening sauces, xii
    what to cook in Instant Pot, xv
Cooking time
    adjusting with "+"/"-," xii
    altitude affecting, xi
    coming to full pressure and, viii
    of recipes. *See specific recipes*
Cornstarch uses, xii
Country Ham Hash, 133
Cranberries
    Caramelized Onion & Cranberry Dip, 7
    Cranberry Spiced Black Tea, 121
    Fresh Cranberry Sauce, 78
    Warm Tropical Punch with a Punch, 126
Creamy Cheesecake with a Touch of Orange, 96–97
Crisping things first, xiii
Crispy Cornish Game Hens for Two, 25

Delay Start button, xii
Desserts, 85–113
    about: Cake button, xi
    Baileys Lava Cakes, 109–110
    Berry Cobbler with Granola Topping, 95
    Chocolate Peanut Butter Buckeyes, 156–157
    Christmas Fudge, 111
    Creamy Cheesecake with a Touch of Orange, 96–97
    It's Actually Really Good Fruitcake, 154–155
    Lemon Curd Tart, 99–100
    Marshmallow Fudge, 167
    Peppermint Bark, 162–163
    Pumpkin Cream Lava Cake, 112–113
    Red Velvet Cheesecake, 104–105
    Seasonal Rice Pudding, 101

Spiced Apple Crisp, 106
Stuffed Cinnamon Walnut Apples, 103
Super-Moist Pumpkin Pie Spice Cake, 90–91
Super-Simple Chocolate Mint Brownies, 93–94
Upside Down, Nutty, Pull-Apart Cinnamon Rolls,
    87–88
Warm Cherries Jubilee, 89
Warm Fruit & Nut Compote, 107
Dessert toppings
    Dulce de Leche, 161
    Homemade Strawberry Jam, 153
    Lemon Curd, 160
Deviled eggs, 12–13
Dips. *See* Appetizers and starters
Display panel, xi
Dressing and stuffing
    Leek, Parsnip & Herb Brioche Dressing, 64–65
    Sausage & Sage Stuffing, 71–72
Drinks, for gifts
    Apple Pie Moonshine, 159
    Classic Limoncello, 151
Drinks, warm, 115–127
    Cranberry Spiced Black Tea, 121
    Dulce de Leche Cider with a Kick, 125
    Hot Buttered Rum, 117
    Kahlúa Vanilla Latte, 127
    Lemon and Rum Hot Toddy, 120
    Peppermint Vanilla Latte, 123
    Spiced & Spiked Hot Cider, 124
    Spiked Hot Chocolate, 119
    Warm Spiced Mulled Wine, 118
    Warm Tropical Punch with a Punch, 126
Duck à l'orange, 35–36
Dulce de Leche, 161
Dulce de Leche Cider with a Kick, 125

Easy Duck à l'Orange, 35–36
Egg button, xi
Eggs, deviled, 12–13
Entrées, 21–51
    Beef Pot Roast, 31
    Beef Stroganoff, 37
    Beer-Braised Shredded Beef, 38
    Colorful Veggie Lasagna, 32–33
    Crispy Cornish Game Hens for Two, 25
    Easy Duck à l'Orange, 35–36
    Pulled Pork, 46

Pumpkin & Sausage Penne, 24
Red Wine–Braised Beef Brisket, 26–27
Roast Pork Loin, 41
Sous Vide Filet Mignon, 47–49
Sous Vide Seared Tuna, 50–51
Steamed Lobster Tails, 39
Succulent Glazed Ham, 22–23
Tender Turkey for a Small Gathering, 29–30
Turkey Breast for Two, 44–45
Venison Roast, 42–43

15-Bean Soup with Ham, 144
Fish and seafood
    Shrimp with Butter & Garlic, 18
    Sous Vide Seared Tuna, 50–51
    Steamed Lobster Tails, 39
Fresh Cranberry Sauce, 78
Fruit. *See also specific fruit*
    It's Actually Really Good Fruitcake, 154–155
    Warm Fruit & Nut Compote, 107
    Warm Tropical Punch with a Punch, 126
Fudge, white chocolate, 111

Gifts, homemade, 149–167
    Apple Pie Moonshine, 159
    Chocolate Peanut Butter Buckeyes, 156–157
    Classic Limoncello, 151
    Dulce de Leche, 161
    Homemade Apple Butter, 164
    Homemade Strawberry Jam, 153
    Homemade Vanilla Extract, 166
    It's Actually Really Good Fruitcake, 154–155
    Lemon Curd, 160
    Marshmallow Fudge, 167
    Peppermint Bark, 162–163
    Sea Salt Popcorn, 152
    Spiced Cashews, 165
Gravy, herb, 74
Green Beans with Toasted Almonds, 75

Ham
    Cheesy Macaroni with Ham, 142–143
    Country Ham Hash, 133
    15-Bean Soup with Ham, 144
    Succulent Glazed Ham, 22–23
Hash, country ham, 133
Herb gravy, 74

Holiday Hummus, 11
Homemade Apple Butter, 164
Homemade Strawberry Jam, 153
Homemade Vanilla Extract, 166
Hot drinks. *See* Drinks, warm
Hummus, 11, 135

Ingredients, brands affecting results, xiv. *See also
    specific main ingredients*
Inner pot, filling and cleaning, xiv
Instant Pot
    altitude cooking times, xi
    buttons, xi–xii
    cleaning inner pot, xiv
    lid holder, xi
    pressure release caution, xi
    silicone rings for, x
    success tips, x. *See also* Cooking suggestions
    time to build pressure, x
It's Actually Really Good Fruitcake, 154–155

Jam, homemade strawberry, 153

Kahlúa Vanilla Latte, 127
Keep Warm button, xii

Latte, Kahlúa vanilla, 127
Latte, peppermint vanilla, 123
Lava cakes, 109–110, 112–113
Leeks
    Leek, Parsnip & Herb Brioche Dressing, 64–65
    Winter Vegetable Mix, 68
Leftovers, 129–147
    Beef & Caramelized Onion Sandwiches, 131–132
    Cheesy Macaroni with Ham, 142–143
    Country Ham Hash, 133
    15-Bean Soup with Ham, 144
    Quick & Easy Turkey Pot Pie, 138
    Sweet Potato Coconut Soup, 137
    Sweet Potato Hummus, 135
    Turkey & Sweet Potato Chili, 139
    Turkey & Wild Rice Soup, 134
    Turkey Bone Broth, 145
    Turkey Marsala, 147
    Turkey Ramen, 140–141
Lemon. *See* Citrus
"Less," "Normal," and "More" indicators, xi

Lid holder, xi
Lobster tails, steamed, 39

Manual button, xii
Marshmallow Fudge, 167
Marshmallows, sweet potatoes and, 57
Mashed potatoes, 73
Meat. *See also specific meat*
    crisping in oven or on grill, xiii
    Meat/Stew button, xi
Meatballs, bourbon-glazed, 17
Milk, in Dulce de Leche, 161
Mint
    Peppermint Vanilla Latte, 123
    Super-Simple Chocolate Mint Brownies, 93–94
"–" and "+" buttons, xii
Moonshine, apple pie, 159
"More," "Less, " and "Normal" indicators, xi
Multigrain button, xii
Mushrooms
    Mushroom Medley, 69
    Tender Stuffed Mushrooms, 5–6

"Normal," "More," and "Less" indicators, xi
No-Soak Black Beans with Ginger & Nutmeg, 83
Nutmeg Spaghetti Squash, 63
Nuts
    about: peanut butter brownie variation, 94
    Chocolate Peanut Butter Buckeyes, 156–157
    Marshmallow Fudge, 167
    Salted Boiled Peanuts, 3
    Spiced Cashews, 165
    Stuffed Cinnamon Walnut Apples, 103
    Upside Down, Nutty, Pull-Apart Cinnamon Rolls,
        87–88
    Warm Fruit & Nut Compote, 107

Onions
    Beef & Caramelized Onion Sandwiches, 131–132
    Caramelized Onion & Cranberry Dip, 7
Orange. *See* Citrus

Parsnips
    Leek, Parsnip & Herb Brioche Dressing, 64–65
    Winter Vegetable Mix, 68
Pasta and pasta alternative
    Cheesy Macaroni with Ham, 142–143

Colorful Veggie Lasagna, 32–33
Nutmeg Spaghetti Squash, 63
Pumpkin & Sausage Penne, 24
Turkey Ramen, 140–141
Pears, in Warm Fruit & Nut Compote, 107
Peppermint Bark, 162–163
Peppermint Vanilla Latte, 123
Pineapple juice, in Warm Tropical Punch with a
    Punch, 126
"+" And "–" buttons, xii
Pomegranate Brussels Sprouts, 66–67
Popcorn, sea salt, 152
Pork. *See also* Ham; Sausage
    about: crisping, xiii; Meat/Stew button, xiii
    Pulled Pork, 46
    Roast Pork Loin, 41
    White Beans with Bacon & Rosemary, 58–59
Porridge button, xii
Potatoes
    Classic Mashed Potatoes, 73
    Country Ham Hash, 133
    Steamed Baby Potatoes with Shallots, 79
    Winter Vegetable Mix, 68
Pot-in-pot cooking, xiv–xv
Pot pie, quick and easy, 138
Poultry
    about: crisping, xiii; Meat/Stew button, xiii
    Asian Chicken Wings, 14–15
    Buffalo Chicken Dip, 8–9
    Crispy Cornish Game Hens for Two, 25
    Easy Duck à l'Orange, 35–36
    Quick & Easy Turkey Pot Pie, 138
    Tender Turkey for a Small Gathering, 29–30
    Turkey & Sweet Potato Chili, 139
    Turkey & Wild Rice Soup, 134
    Turkey Breast for Two, 44–45
    Turkey Marsala, 147
    Turkey Ramen, 140–141
Pressure
    coming to full, viii
    natural release, xiii
    protecting cabinets from, xi
    quick release, xiii
    silicone rings for airtight seal, x
    slow release, xiii
Pressure Cook button, xii
Pressure Level button, xii

Pulled Pork, 46
Pumpkin
    Pumpkin & Sausage Penne, 24
    Pumpkin Cream Lava Cake, 112–113
    Savory Pumpkin Risotto, 61
    Super-Moist Pumpkin Pie Spice Cake, 90–91
Punch, warm tropical, 126

Quick & Easy Turkey Pot Pie, 138

Red Velvet Cheesecake, 104–105
Red Wine–Braised Beef Brisket, 26–27
Rice and wild rice
    about: Rice button, xii
    Savory Pumpkin Risotto, 61
    Seasonal Rice Pudding, 101
    Turkey & Wild Rice Soup, 134
Roast Pork Loin, 41
Rum. *See* Drinks, warm

Salted Boiled Peanuts, 3
Sandwiches, beef & caramelized onion, 131–132
Sauces
    about: thickening with cornstarch, xii
    Apple-Orange Chutney, 77
    Chunky Cinnamon Applesauce, 56
    Easy Herb Gravy, 74
    Fresh Cranberry Sauce, 78
    Homemade Apple Butter, 164
    Homemade Strawberry Jam, 153
Sausage
    Pumpkin & Sausage Penne, 24
    Sausage & Sage Stuffing, 71–72
    Sweet & Spicy Cocktail Sausages, 19
Sauté button, xii, xv
Savory Pumpkin Risotto, 61
Seafood. *See* Fish and seafood
Sea Salt Popcorn, 152
Seasonal Rice Pudding, 101
Shrimp with Butter & Garlic, 18
Sides, 53–83
    Acorn Squash with Shallots & Grapes, 55
    The Best Beet Salad, 81–82
    Cauliflower Au Gratin, 62
    Chunky Cinnamon Applesauce, 56
    Classic Mashed Potatoes, 73
    Easy Herb Gravy, 74

Sides *(cont.)*
    Fresh Cranberry Sauce, 78
    Green Beans with Toasted Almonds, 75
    Leek, Parsnip & Herb Brioche Dressing, 64–65
    Mushroom Medley, 69
    No-Soak Black Beans with Ginger & Nutmeg, 83
    Nutmeg Spaghetti Squash, 63
    Pomegranate Brussels Sprouts, 66–67
    Sausage & Sage Stuffing, 71–72
    Savory Pumpkin Risotto, 61
    Steamed Baby Potatoes with Shallots, 79
    Sweet Potatoes & Marshmallows, 57
    White Beans with Bacon & Rosemary, 58–59
    Winter Vegetable Mix, 68
Silicone rings, x
Slow Cook button, xii
Soups, stews, and chili
    about: Bean/Chili button, xi; Soup/Broth button, xi
    15-Bean Soup with Ham, 144
    Sweet Potato Coconut Soup, 137
    Turkey & Sweet Potato Chili, 139
    Turkey & Wild Rice Soup, 134
    Turkey Bone Broth, 145
Sous vide cooking, xv
Sous Vide Filet Mignon, 47–49
Sous Vide Seared Tuna, 50–51
Spice cake, super-moist pumpkin pie, 90–91
Spiced & Spiked Hot Cider, 124
Spiced Apple Crisp, 106
Spiced Cashews, 165
Spiced mulled wine, warm, 118
Spiked Hot Chocolate, 119
Spinach, in Warm & Creamy Spinach Artichoke
    Dip, 10
Squash
    Acorn Squash with Shallots & Grapes, 55
    Nutmeg Spaghetti Squash, 63
Steam button, xii
Steamed Baby Potatoes with Shallots, 79
Steamed Lobster Tails, 39
Sterilize button, xii
Strawberry jam, homemade, 153
Stuffed Cinnamon Walnut Apples, 103
Stuffing. *See* Dressing and stuffing
Success tips, x
Succulent Glazed Ham, 22–23
Super-Moist Pumpkin Pie Spice Cake, 90–91

Super-Simple Chocolate Mint Brownies, 93–94
Sweet & Spicy Cocktail Sausages, 19
Sweet potatoes
    Sweet Potato Coconut Soup, 137
    Sweet Potatoes & Marshmallows, 57
    Sweet Potato Hummus, 135
    Turkey & Sweet Potato Chili, 139

Tea, cranberry spiced black, 121
Tender Stuffed Mushrooms, 5–6
Tender Turkey for a Small Gathering, 29–30
Tuna, sous vide seared, 50–51
Turkey. *See* Poultry
Turkey Bone Broth, 145

Upside Down, Nutty, Pull-Apart Cinnamon Rolls,
    87–88

Vanilla
    Homemade Vanilla Extract, 166
    Kahlúa Vanilla Latte, 127
    Peppermint Vanilla Latte, 123
Vegetables. *See also* Sides; specific vegetables
    Colorful Veggie Lasagna, 32–33
    Winter Vegetable Mix, 68
Venison Roast, 42–43

Walnuts. *See* Nuts
Warm & Creamy Spinach Artichoke Dip, 10
Warm Brie with Honey & Apples, 2
Warm Cherries Jubilee, 89
Warm Fruit & Nut Compote, 107
Warm Spiced Mulled Wine, 118
Warm Tropical Punch with a Punch, 126
White chocolate fudge, 111
Wine, warm spiced mulled, 118
Winter Vegetable Mix, 68

Yogurt button, xii